A HISTORY OF
THE PILGRIMS' SCHOOL

A History of
THE PILGRIMS' SCHOOL
and
arlier Winchester choir schools

JOHN CROOK

Phillimore

© 1991

Published by
PHILLIMORE & CO. LTD.
Shopwyke Hall, Chichester, Sussex

© John Crook, 1991

ISBN 0 85033 809 3

Phototypeset in 11/12 pt Baskerville by
INTYPE, London
Printed and bound in Great Britain by
BIDDLES LTD.
Guildford, Surrey

CONTENTS

LIST OF PLATES

PREFACE

SIXTY YEARS AGO the Dean of Winchester, Edward Gordon Selwyn, and the Chapter decided to make different arrangements for the education of the 20 Cathedral Choristers who, until that time, had lived a nomadic existence around the Close and its immediate vicinity. They decided that these were now to become part of a normal preparatory school, which would grow to a usual size – about 60 boys in those days – and have the use of normal preparatory school facilities. This was quite an innovative move for those times, when most choir schools tended to be small, insular and educationally isolated.

Members of the Chapter selected as the site for this bold experiment the buildings of No.3 The Close, and then in their infinite wisdom they chose Humphrey and Lorna Salwey to be the first management team for the instruction of their infant prodigy. The name for the new school was taken from that of the Hall adjacent to the main school building. This imposing medieval construction was then being used as a store room, but had originally been designed – so the fable ran – to shelter pilgrims visiting the shrine of St Swithun or about to embark on the journey to Canterbury along the Pilgrims' Way. So the new creation became The Pilgrims' School and its numbers slowly increased, first boarders and then dayboys, with new buildings at regular intervals, two of them named after the original founders of the school – Selwyn and Salwey – and another after a benevolent and entirely supportive Dean, Michael Stancliffe. The final major addition to the numerical strength came in 1966, when the Quiristers of Winchester College became officially incorporated following a formal agreement between the Dean and Chapter and the Warden and Fellows. So the school settled into its present union of Choristers, Quiristers and Commoners, unusual for its history, its foundation, its musical enrichment and, increasingly as years went by, for its lack of girls and pre-prep department. So The Pilgrims' has survived, and indeed flourished, as a traditional preparatory school, solely for the education of boys, but far from being an exclusive enclave of masculinity, thanks to the strong and most welcome influence of many generations of devoted lady members of staff.

When the school celebrated its Golden Jubilee 10 years ago, John Crook very kindly volunteered his services to write a comprehensive history of the present school and its antecedents. Now, 10 years later, he has, with equal kindness, agreed to up-date the original work, to incorporate the events of the last decade. We are indeed fortunate that he should do this because, splendid though the first volume was, several significant events have happened since its publication and it seems in every way fitting that these should be recorded so that the history of this very unusual school should be brought, as far as possible, up to date.

History must be a subject which involves every person who enters The Pilgrims', whether as teacher, parent or pupil. One cannot but be aware of the enormous influence of previous generations who constructed the Pilgrims' Hall and the many other buildings which comprise the school now. They had a mind and a purpose in their building, which we are fortunate to inherit. When Her Royal Highness The Princess Margaret came to open the newest addition, the Stancliffe Building, in 1989, it seemed in every way appropriate that the reading at the service should be from St Paul's first letter to the Corinthians (3: 10–17), which contains the words, 'like a skilled master-builder I laid a foundation and another man is building upon it'. As these words were read by the Head Commoner, it brought home to me the fact that we were all assembled in the shadow of the school founded by Dean Selwyn and Humphrey Salwey, in a building said to have been designed by Sir Christopher Wren, and to which additions have been made and will be made by successive pupils, teachers and headmasters. We must be appreciative of our past and feel linked to it by generations of Old Pilgrims and former members of staff; these are the links which carry us back to our foundation, and a rich inheritance they pass on to us, as I am daily aware. This book helps to remind us of that debt, especially owed to Humphrey and Lorna Salwey, now sadly no longer with us, but who have left such an indelible reminder of their presence in the world. *Si monumentum requiris* indeed!

The school is lucky to have such good neighbours in the College and the Cathedral; they give us daily enrichment, as do the boys who pass through the doors of The Pilgrims', contributing to its life and well-being. I hope they will always be as proud to have been associated with The Pilgrims' as I shall be, and that if they need any reminder in years to come, they will blow the dust off this book and remember with gratitude all that lies within it – *forsan et haec olim meminisse iuvabit*.

M. E. K. KEFFORD

December 1990

The publication of this revised edition was made possible through the extreme generosity of an anonymous donor to whom we offer our grateful thanks.

Part I

THE LIFE AND EDUCATION OF WINCHESTER CATHEDRAL CHORISTERS BEFORE 1931

Chapter One

FROM THE DARK AGES TO THE COMMONWEALTH

EVEN THE MOST VENERABLE of institutions may be subject to the temptation of claiming greater antiquity than the surviving historical records actually allow. At the individual level, this trend may be seen in the modern popularity of genealogy, the search for 'roots': all must have an illustrious, or at least a lengthy, pedigree, however many side-steps in the family tree this may involve. Those who have traced the history of our Choir and its associated schools have sometimes yielded to the same temptation; such as the late Canon Goodman, who considered Winchester's Anglo-Saxon 'Grammar School', the *Alta Schola*, 'a kind of collateral ancestor of the Pilgrims' School'.[1]

The claim seems exaggerated. The *Alta Schola* was certainly the earliest recorded school in Winchester: it was established on a site west of the Cathedral, perhaps as early as the seventh century, when the West Saxon bishopric was transferred to Winchester from Dorchester upon Thames. According to Bishop Asser, the youngest son of Alfred the Great was sent to school there; and it is even said that Alfred himself was a pupil. However, there is no true connection between the later choir schools and the *Alta Schola* (which survived until the reforms of Henry VIII), and any suggestion that Alfred might be claimed as the first Old Pilgrim is merely an entertaining fantasy.

A more fruitful ground for investigation is the monastic *schola* or Novices' School of the Anglo-Saxon Old Minster, after the 10th-century monastic reform. As A. F. Leach emphasises in his classic *History of Winchester College*,[2] there is no clear link between this school and the arrangements made for the general education of our Choristers from the 15th century; nevertheless, it seems probable that from the late 10th century youths from the *schola* formed the choir which sang in the Saxon Minster, until at a later date this task was taken on by boys from the Almonry of St Swithun's Priory.

Some idea of the duties of the Novices may be gained from *Regularis Concordia*, compiled by Bishop Ethelwold in 970. This monastic code of custom was not written uniquely for Winchester; but it is likely that its precepts were closely observed in the church where it was composed. The *pueri* evidently played an important part in the devotional life of the foundation, starting in the earliest hours of the morning, when 'the entire *schola* with their master and the abbot

3

shall wash their faces as is customary, intent on the psalms as they do so'.[3] As well as participating in the daily offices, the *pueri* were required to carry out other duties on specific days in the church calendar: to sing Theodulf of Orleans' famous hymn on Palm Sunday; to read the Resurrection narrative on Holy Saturday, and the Nativity story at Christmas; and to take turns in the daily distribution of alms to the poor – first the 'right-hand choir', then the 'left-hand choir'; for singing then as now was performed by a double choir, a feature of Benedictine ritual that has survived in the Anglican church.

The injunctions of *Regularis Concordia* are prescriptive rather than descriptive: we learn nothing of the specific musical practices of Winchester. Another text seems to provide more information about the Saxon Minster's organ: it is described, with considerable licence, in the *Poem of the Cantor Wulfstan* dating from about the year 990. It is said of this instrument that, when it played, folk in the streets of Winchester stopped their ears in amazement. 'Like thunder the iron voice assaults the ear, driving out every other sound.'[4] According to Wulfstan, this musical monster had 400 pipes and 26 bellows operated by 70 strong men working like galley-slaves, and was played by two monks, each at his keyboard. Unfortunately, it is now thought that these details are mere poetic exaggeration.

Interesting though the *Winchester Troper*[5] may be in the history of the development of polyphony, with its collection of *organa* in one of the surviving manuscripts, there is nothing to suggest that boys' voices were needed or employed in its 11th-century sequences and tropes.

It is indeed a further 300 years before explicit references to singing in Winchester are found, by which time the Saxon Minster had been replaced by the great Norman church of Walkelin. In 1301 Bishop John of Pontoise founded the College of St Elizabeth of Hungary '*in prato nostro quod est ante portam castri nostri de Wolveseie*':* [6] the foundations of the chapel may still be distinguished in this meadow, to the south-east of New Hall. Each of the six chaplains there was accompanied by a surpliced singing-boy, aged 10 to 18: '*Habeat quilibet capellanus unum clericulum a decem annis usque ad decimum octavum annum qui in ecclesia in superpellicio cantet et legat et sibi in camera deserviat . . .*'† Meanwhile in the Priory, the Novices' School had dwindled, and the *schola* could not provide singing-boys in the numbers implied by *Regularis Concordia*. Perhaps the very practice of boys' singing had fallen into disuse. We cannot tell. There were certainly boys of a suitable age within the monastery precincts, both in the Novices' School and in the Almonry. Some idea of their number may be obtained from the Compotus Rolls giving details of the day-to-day expenses noted by the various monastic officials or 'obedientiaries': the boys in the Novices' School, for example, used to receive a shilling knife every year from the Almoner or Hordarian. Thus we know that in 1382 there were three boys in the school: '*Item: iij Iuvenibus in scola existentibus pro eorum cultellis iij*ˢ'.§[7] However, we are more concerned with the Almonry boys at this date; for as at Canterbury (from 1321), so in Winchester, it was from the charity boys of the Almonry that our first recorded Choristers were drawn.

One date which was eagerly awaited by choristers throughout Europe in the

---

* 'in our meadow which is in front of the gate of our castle of Wolvesey'
† 'Each chaplain will have a "clerklet" aged 10 to 18, who will sing and read in the church, wearing a surplice, and will serve him in his chamber'.
§ 'Item: to the 3 boys now in the school for their knives: 3/-'

Middle Ages was the feast of St Nicholas (6 December) on whose eve one of their number would be elected 'Boy Bishop', and for three weeks would lord it not only over his peers but over the grown-ups as well! The whole exercise was a practical application of the phrase 'He hath put down the mighty from their seat' and a reminder of the Psalmist's words, echoed in the Holy Innocents' Day introit: '*Ex ore infantium*' (Psalm 8: 3). It was probably more fun for the boys than for the adults, who must have breathed a sigh of relief when Childermas, 28 December, had passed, and the high Saturnalia was over for another year.

At Winchester the Boy Bishop was chosen from the Almonry boys, and William Waynflete specified that one of the duties of the Curtarian at St Swithun's Priory was to provide four dishes of meat for the boys during their merry-making: '*Curtarius administrabit infantibus quatuor diebus Natalis Domini quatuor fercula carnium*';*[8] and on the last day the boys were given an issue of wine or beer. In 1312 the beer cost 3½d. as the Roll of Adam of Hyde shows: '*In cervisia missa Iuvenum Episcopo die Innocentium iij^dob*'.†[9]

It seems likely that these well-feasted Almonry boys were already being used as Choristers. But perhaps the origins of our present Choir may be found earlier than this: in the construction of the Lady Chapel in around 1200 by Bishop Godfrey de Lucy. The cult of the Blessed Virgin Mary, which spread from the Orient throughout the whole of Western Christendom during the 12th century, had a wide-ranging influence on the arts: on architecture, with the erection of churches and chapels dedicated to the Holy Mother; on the associated decorative arts of sculpture and painting; and on literature, where a softer, more feminine society was reflected in the courtly romances and Ovidian fantasies of authors like Chrétien de Troyes. Music usually seems to be the last of the arts to follow cultural trends; but the new devotion to Our Lady gradually took musical form, and boys came to be employed in Lady Chapel choirs, where their unbroken voices suggested a gentler, appropriately feminine, religious atmosphere. From the 13th century date the first Marian Masses dedicated to Our Lady, and the Marian Antiphons proper to the changing seasons of the Church's year: *Alma Redemptoris Mater, Ave Regina, Regina Coeli* and *Salve Regina*.

By deduction and analogy with other cathedrals, we may tentatively speculate that boys' voices were heard in our own Cathedral as early as the beginning of the 13th century. Certainly the office of Precentor existed at that time, although there is no evidence to suggest that his musical functions consisted of anything more than acting as 'Cantor' and leading the monks in plainsong in the main Cathedral Quire. Indeed, it is quite clear that the boys' choir, when it first appeared, was a separate body from that of the monks; and it is interesting to note that the term 'Children of the Chapel' (i.e. the Lady Chapel) survives as late as 1539 to denote our Choristers.

One of the Almoner's Rolls, dated 1317, has a rather uncertain reference to an Organist; but the first actual name dates from nearly a century later, and is contained in Winchester Cathedral's first *Ledger Book*: these books are a valuable source of information about the life of the Cathedral from the beginning of the 15th century. On 29 September 1402 John Tyes was appointed Organist and

---

* 'The Curtarian will give the children four dishes of meat on the four days of the Nativity of Our Lord'
† 'For beer sent to the Boy Bishop on Holy Innocents' Day, 3½d.'

Choirmaster: he was 'to be of service to the convent by playing the organ and singing at the daily mass of Blessed Mary which is said at the altar of the same name . . . and by instructing the convent boys in chant on the understanding that their number will never exceed four'.[10] For this he received eight silver Marks a year and a fur-trimmed robe, the use of a room and the privilege of dining with the Prior in the Prior's Hall at major feasts and whenever he had played the organ. John Tyes was evidently an influential character in Winchester. We know that he leased a cottage and an adjacent barn belonging to the Priory in 'Beggar-street',*[11] his name also occurs in the *Winchester Black Book* kept by the Corporation of Winchester in the 15th century: a *Memorandum* dated 1419 mentions that he had lately been re-elected a 'citizen' and that in consideration of his various responsibilities within the Priory of St Swithun, in the Chapel of the Blessed Virgin Mary (and the payment of £3), he was to be let off jury service and other civic duties.[12] Unfortunately, rather less is known of his activities in the Monastery church.

The small number of Choristers in the care of John Tyes need not surprise us. At the neighbouring cathedral of Salisbury only two choristers sang at a time during the weekday offices, enabling their colleagues to attend their lessons; but the small number at Winchester may equally well indicate that our boys were by this date beginning to sing in chorus with the monks, singing descants or other independently-written musical lines known as 'Prycksong' as opposed to plain-song: another step on the road to polyphony, whose germ we have noted in the *Winchester Troper*. No doubt the musical education given to our singing-boys (and to the pupils of the *Alta Schola* who, by episcopal decree, were to learn music once they had mastered the reading of the psalter)[13] would enable them to read the comparatively new *Ars Nova* notation as well as the neumes of plainchant. It seems likely that the merging of the two choirs, so separate in their physical location within the great church, was a gradual process.

Before he died, William of Wykeham had come to an agreement with Prior Thomas Neville, which took effect from 16 August 1404, that 'the boys living in the almonry school of the priory will, after the bishop's death, sing the antiphon *Salve Regina* or the *Ave Regina* every evening in his chapel'.[14] For these services in his chantry chapel in the Cathedral they received 6s. 8d. *per annum*.

Our next reference to the Choristers dates from 1482, when Edmund Pynbrygge was appointed Master of the Choristers, though on rather more favourable terms than Tyes: he was paid a salary of 10 Marks (£6.67) and was allowed to dine daily in the Prior's Hall, as well as receiving three yards of broadcloth each year for his gown. His task was 'yearly and daily to inform, instruct and teach all the boys of the Prior and Convent now serving, or hereafter to serve, in the choir of the church at the time of divine service, in chant and descant, to the number of eight or less, never more'.[15] It will be noticed that the Lady Chapel is not mentioned and that the boys' singing activities now specifically include descants. With the development of polyphony, the boys' choir has doubled in size. It seems that Pynbrygge was not the Organist: successive Organists frequently delegated their responsibility for training and educating the Choristers.

From this period come the first, tantalisingly brief glimpses into the Choristers'

---

* He appears to have lived on the corner of Lower Brook Street and Silver Hill.

daily life. In November 1486, Henry VII visited Winchester for Prince Arthur's baptism. According to Thomas Warton, he dined at the Castle and 'was entertained with a religious drama called *Christi descensus ad inferno*. It was represented by the *pueri eleemosynarii* or choir-boys of Hyde Abbey and St Swithun's Priory'.[16] It was Henry VII who was responsible for the transfer of Bishop Langton from Salisbury to Winchester in 1493: Langton was a good musician and started a school in the palace precincts, where youths were trained in grammar and music. Equally important was his concern for the education of the monks: in 1497 Peter Druett, a lay-man, was appointed to teach the monks grammar. There is no actual evidence that he taught the singing-boys, but his youthful servant used to dine at the Chapel Boys' table, which might hint at a connection.[17]

Pynbrygge retired in 1510 and Thomas Goodman succeeded him as master of the 'Children of the Chapel of Blessed Mary'. As well as teaching not more than ten boys singing, he was to sing himself, and also play the organ.[18] In 1538 a similar agreement was made with Matthew Fuller: at a salary of £4.33, seven loaves and seven gallons of beer a week, but apparently no Prior's Hall dinners![19] It was now the eve of the Dissolution of the Priory, and a sign of the increased secularisation of such foundations may perhaps be seen in the fact that in the same year as Fuller became Organist a grammar-school master was appointed to 'teach the children of the chapell & the children of the Almnary with a pension of £3 and diet in the Prior's hall with the Sellarrer and four broad yards of cloath & also a chamber, [...] six bottles of the best ale every week & seven loaves'.[20] The separation of the Almonry and the Choristers' 'School' was evidently complete.

The Priory of St Swithun was dissolved in November 1539, and, after a 17-month interval, the former Prior, William Basing, was installed at the head of his newly formed Chapter as Dean William Kingsmill. Under the Cathedral Statutes, dated 1541, there were to be 12 Lay Clerks and 10 Choristers, '*pueri tenerae aetatis et vocibus sonoris ad cantandum aptis*'.*[21] One of the 12 Lay Clerks, 'of honest repute and uncorrupt life, skilled in singing and playing the organ', was to train the boys. Richard Wynslade became the first such Organist and Master of the Choristers, and Matthew Fuller joined the then ageing Thomas Goodman as a mere Lay Clerk, at a starting salary of £6 13s. 8d. *per annum*.[22]

With the closure of the monastery, alternative accommodation had to be provided for the Choristers. The Treasurers' Rolls dating from immediately after the Reformation show that the Organist was also in charge of the Choristers' house in the Close: for example, in 1541 Richard Wynslade received £8 6s. 8d. 'pro the dyette, rayment and other necessarys pro the same choristars' plus a further 20s. 'for the co[o]kes wages servying the same choristars'.[23] One of the other Lay Vicars or 'syngingmen', William Way, appears to have acted as Wynslade's assistant and received an annual stipend of 6s. 8d. for 'repeting in the quier'.[24] Various details may be gleaned from the Treasurer's Roll for the following year: the rent paid by Wynslade for the 'children's house', the cost of sundry repairs, including a 'chimney-mantell'; the price (8s.) of 'one bedde and coverlett and a payer of blanketes & a paer of shetes'.[25]

A vestige of monasticism which had survived the Reformation was the tonsuring of Choristers. One of the first actions of Edward VI on ascending the throne was

* 'Boys of tender years and with resonant voices suitable for singing'

to put a stop to this practice by Royal Injunction: '*Item*: that all maner of coristars of this sayde chirche shall from hensforthe suffer their Crownes to growe and be no more shaven butt onely ther heare to be rowndede and clypped short'.[26] Other equally practical injunctions were sent to the Dean and Chapter in the following decades by Bishop Horne: as well as giving specific orders about the need for clear pronunciation when singing, he commanded that the Choristers should be taught and examined in 'the Catechism in English written by Mr Nowell, Dean of Pawles' and 'shall further learn to read and write of their teacher or some such as shall be by the Dean and Chapter provided'.[27]

Perhaps the most valuable post-Reformation documents available to researchers studying the Cathedral's past are the Chapter Books, where, in addition to Chapter Orders, minutes and *memoranda*, the names of all members of the General Chapter are inscribed at the twice-yearly Chapter meetings. Dean Young described the procedure in his *Diary*: 'Efter the collects we goe oup to the chaptour house. Then the psalme God be merciful unto us etc., and the prayer for the King etc., then names called; then I spake to the Queer, then we dismisse them and go to chouse our officers'.[28] Chapter meetings have changed little since that extract was written, on 25 November 1631, and they were no doubt considered as much of an irksome chore by 17th-century Choristers as they are now: a sense of historical perspective takes time to develop! There is a gap in the series of Chapter Books from 1601 to 1621; but one of Winchester's best-known Choristers found another way of preserving his name for posterity: he carved it, 'ADRIAN:BAT-TIN:1608', in the stonework of Bishop Gardiner's chantry chapel. Such acts, which nowadays would be classified as vandalism, were apparently not restricted to the choir-boys: a few years later the Organist, Thomas Holmes, also left his name on one of the Nave pillars!

Just where the Choristers were lodged in the 16th century remains a mystery. It is likely that their song-school moved about the Close with the Organist: in the 1590s, when Canon Bennett was granted the use of the 'Common Hall', he had to sign an undertaking that he would make a room available for the Choristers to be lodged or taught in if necessary.[29] However, in the early 17th century the Organist George Bath probably lived in rooms over the porter's lodge, and kept his song-school there. In 1626 he was granted the use of a 'Cellar' in part of the present Pilgrims' School buildings,[30] although the purpose of this room is not specified. George Bath may have acted as Housemaster to his Choristers, for the Treasurer's Roll of 1627 mentions the payment of £40 13s. 4d. '*pro hospitium choristarum*'[31] – a substantial sum. Singing-boys were probably lodged in the Close until the disruption caused by the Parliamentary occupation of the cathedral precincts created an acute housing shortage at the Restoration.

For nearly two centuries after the return of the Monarchy, almost all the Choristers may have been dayboys: a study of post-Restoration Choristers' names suggests that singing was very much a local and indeed a family affair: Choristers were sons of Lay Vicars, bell-ringers, porters, virgers and other Cathedral officers; and often graduated to lay clerk status themselves once their voices broke. The family names recur as one brother after another passes through the choir. Availability was probably the most powerul consideration when selecting Choristers, and the resulting musical standards may not have been high.

However, one favourable review has survived from this period. In August 1634 a 'Lieutenant of the Military Company in Norwich' and his companion 'tumbled down a steepy hill a whole mile together into that ancient city of Winchester':[32] they were spending their term of leave on a tour of the West Country. Lieutenant Hammond – for so he has been identified – wrote a full account of his visit to Winchester. The Quire-stalls with their elaborate carvings, and other architectural features of the Cathedral, seem to have interested our Lieutenant more than the music, but he observed that 'the Organs in this church are not exceedingly fair nor rich, but sweet and tunable, and sweetly played on by one of the rarest organists† that this land affords, who is now of his Maiesties Chappel. The Quiristers were skilfull, and the voices good, when they sing sweet and heavenly anthems.'[33]

A better-known visitor to the Cathedral in the same year as Lieutenant Hammond was Archbishop Laud. Among other questions in his searching enquiry into church discipline, he asked 'whether the boys be suffered to play in the cathedral church-yard whereby windows are sometimes broken'.[34] Over a hundred years previously, Canon Denton, of St George's Chapel, Windsor, had grappled with the same problem, recommending 'sharp correction and beatings' for offenders.[35] Three years later Laud sent a draft of the proposed new Cathedral Statutes to the Dean and Chapter, asking for their comments. The Chapter's main concern for the Choir was that it was too large and the salaries of the Lay Vicars too small, so that they were lured away by churches that paid their singers better; they asked for the Choir to be reduced in size.[36] Thus, by the Caroline Statutes of 1638, the number of Lay Vicars was reduced to 10, and the number of Choristers to six.[37] Little is said in the Statutes about the general education of the singing-boys: Laud apparently did not regard the choir school as falling within the scope of these injunctions. Nevertheless the Organist, apparently supernumerary to the 10 Lay Vicars, was now 'to train these boys and imbue them with modesty of manners, as well as in skill of song and in playing cunningly upon instruments of music'.[38]

There is only one indication that this last-mentioned broadening of the boys' musical education was put into effect: a post-Restoration Chapter Order 'that a Guitarre not exceeding fourty shillings to be bought for Corfe ye Chorister'.[39] In fact the Treasurer's records a year later show that the 'Gittar and Strings' cost £2 2s. 6d.,[40] and Corfe's musical activities put the Chapter to some further expense in February 1685, when a 'bundle of Gittar strings' was provided for him, at a cost of 8s.[41]

Dean Young's *Diary* relates that from 25 June 1638 the offices of 'Organist' and 'Master of the Choristers' were shared among two Lay Clerks. 'I admitted Jo. Silver Mr. of the Queresters and singing man, and Ch. Gibbons* organist and singing man.'[42] This was the eve of the Commonwealth. Four years later, on 12 December 1642, the Parliamentary soldiers entered the Church: 'they burnt the Books of Common Prayer and all the singing books belonging to the Quire. They throw down the Organs . . .'[43] Music in the church ceased, the Close was more or less abandoned, and for a time there was a very real fear that the Cathedral itself might be demolished.

† Thomas Holmes
* Christopher Gibbons, son of Orlando

Chapter Two

FROM THE RESTORATION TO THE END OF THE NINETEENTH CENTURY

ON 29 MAY 1660 Charles II returned to London. The new Dean of Winchester, Alexander Hyde, was appointed four months later; the Prebendaries moved back into the Close, and the business of repairing the Cathedral and the Close buildings began. Christopher Gibbons took up his post as Organist once again (he had joined the Royalist army in 1644), but he did not stay in Winchester for long. A more prestigious position awaited him at Westminster Abbey and he left for London, just as Thomas Holmes, his predecessor, had done. In 1661 John Silver, already Master of the Choristers, took over the duties of Organist.

Before the Commonwealth John Silver had lived above the porter's lodge next to the building now known as Cheyney Court (the name originally applied only to one low room used by the Bishop for judicial procedures). At the Restoration his house was leased to one Lancelott Barrows; but the terms of his Indenture with the Dean and Chapter specifically excluded the 'Cheyney Court', the porter's rooms and 'ye roome up a paire of staires high over ye said lodge and next ye gallery thence towards ye Close [. . .] for the use of the Master of ye Choristers [. . .] to keepe his song school there'.[1] The lease was renewed under similar terms eight years later, by which time the 'gallery' had been demolished.

No doubt there were considerable difficulties in establishing the Choir again after a 15-year break. Traditions of singing had been suspended and had to be learned anew by the boys: in some cathedrals the choral services were maintained by men's voices alone for a time after 1660. John Silver appears to have subscribed to Dr. Edward Lowe's *Directions for performance of Cathedrall service*, published soon after the Restoration. A further difficulty was that Winchester was without an organ for several years: Thomas Thamer agreed to set up the Choir organ by Christmas 1665 and the Great organ was rebuilt by Renatus Harris in 1694 and survived until the mid-19th century.

Following Laud's example, Archbishop Juxon made a 'visitation' of the Cathedral in 1662 and enquired 'who hath the charge of catechising and instructing [the Choristers] in the principles of Religion?', to which the Chapter replied that 'the statutes of the Church appoynteth a master to teach the choristers musick and to breed them in good manners'.[2] The Treasurer's Rolls show that from 1697 a former Lay Clerk, Mr. Box, received £2 a year for teaching the Choristers their catechism;[3] but we do not know who was responsible for this in the 1660s.

Another setback was to affect the Choir just when Thomas Thamer's organ was near to completion: the Plague. From June 1666 'chanting services' ceased 'by reason of the great increase of the sickness within the City of Winton and the suburbs thereof',[4] and the members of the Chapter removed to Alresford. It seems likely that John Silver was himself a victim: in November, his daughter was ordered 'to deliver all ye singing books late in her father's custody to such persons as ye Deane [. . .] shall appoint':[5] the Chapter had the books fumigated as the Treasurer's entry shows 'pro fumigando Libr. Music. 2/6d'.[6]

Silver's successor, Randolf Jewett, was probably the first to try out the new organ: he was, however, quickly succeeded by John Reading, whose Responses are still sung in the Cathedral. Reading appears to have been irascible rather than conscientious, and soon after his appointment was reprimanded 'for giving undue and oversevere correction to some of the Choristers' and warned 'to take greater care and diligence in the improvement of the Choristers in Musick than hitherto he hath done'.[7] Three years later he was replaced by Daniel Roseingrave, a pupil of Purcell. Reading became Organist of Winchester College, where he is credited with composing the song Dulce Domum. It seems an inappropriate choice, but perhaps his savage temper had sweetened somewhat by then.

The Chapter accounts of the period suggest that one of Daniel Roseingrave's first actions was to create a reasonably comfortable 'singing school'. This was probably no more than a single practice room; as we have suggested, the Choristers from the Restoration to the 19th century were mostly dayboys, often the sons of Cathedral employees. The regular payments of 'Chimney Money' (Hearth Tax) and the amounts involved show that the 'school' was heated by a single hearth: the Dean and Chapter provided 5s. worth of 'coales' annually.

In 1682, the year after Roseingrave's appointment, the Dean and Chapter expended £1 5s. 9d. on various necessaries for the 'school': 'window curtaines, curtaine rodds, [fire] dogs & chairs etc'.[8] And as well as providing the Choristers with a modicum of comfort, the Chapter also paid for some amusements: the same Treasurer's Roll contains the entry, 'A bonfire to ye choristers, 5th November [1683]'.[9]

The boys' practice room may well have been more comfortable than it had been formerly; but the wording of a Chorister's contract, dated 1690, suggests that it was difficult to enforce attendance of the boys there: the Chapter had already ordered that 'none shalbe received or continued choristers in this Church but such as according to Statute come to be duely instructed and educated both in singing & good manners by ye Master of ye Choristers'.[10] The text of the contract gave binding force to this decision: 'the said John Byrom shall from time to time and at all times hereafter be constantly at Morning and Evening prayer at the said Church and shall daily be at the Singing School of Mr Daniel Roseingrave [. . .] at such hours and times as he shall appoint'.[11]

From this period date the first benevolent attempts to make provision for the future of the Choristers once their voices had broken. True, some favoured Choristers had received help in the past; Dean Young mentions in his Diary how he assisted one youth: 'The boy Jenings put out, and I promised at the audit next to healpe him somewhat to put him to a trade: 20/- they go of'.[12] However, there are no references to a regular leaving gratuity until 1667, when it was decided that 'for the better encouragement of our present Choristers and the Parentes of such youthes as are fitt to be trayned upp in singing [. . .] the sum of £8 shalbe annually sett apart [. . .] for the binding them out to be Apprentices' or some other 'way of settlement for their future advantage'.[13] It cost £6 per boy to apprentice Choristers in the 17th century, but by the mid-19th century the apprentice fee appears to have risen to as much as £30: the system was discarded shortly afterwards. Apprenticeship to an organist provided one of the few ways of becoming a professional musician in the 17th century. In 1685 Daniel Roseingrave took 'Chorister George' to his apprentice and received £5 from the Chapter to help clothe the boy;[14] and a similar arrangement was made when his successor, Vaughan Richardson, took on 'Broadway the Chorister'.[15] Many years later, in 1812, an experiment was made of having all the boys bound apprentice to the Organist, perhaps to give him greater legal power over them; but this scheme was abandoned at the end of a year.

Cathedral music continued in desultory fashion. There is no attendance record from the early years of the 18th century, but Vaughan Richardson and his successor John Bishop worked with nine Lay Clerks and five to six Choristers at the most. In some years the number of boys entered in the Chapter Books dwindled to as few as four. The salary scale was hardly encouraging: 55 guineas *per annum* for the Organist, £2 13s. 4d. for each Chorister and £13 10s. per Lay Vicar. The latter sum was fixed by statute and became absurdly small in the 19th century when it was supplemented by a complex system of 'rewards' for attendance.

In 1742 the Choristers' studies were widened somewhat: 'Ordered that after Xmas next the six choristers shall be put to school to Mr Holloway to learn reading, writing and arithmetic'[16] – for which services Mr. Holloway received £6 *per annum*. A paltry sum; but the wording of the Chapter Act suggests that this instruction took place in an established school outside the Close.

By this time James Kent had begun his long tenure of office as Organist: he had himself been a Chorister at Winchester from 1712. He supplemented his income from the Chapter by holding the post of College Organist at the same time, and was praised by a contemporary Warden for being 'conscientiously diligent in the more laborious and indispensable parts of an organist's duty, the teaching of the boys'.[17]

One of his most talented pupils was Charles Dibdin, who joined the Cathedral Choir in 1756, at the age of 11. His voice soon attracted the attention of a wider public than the Cathedral congregation alone. 'The Winchester concert-rooms at the races and assizes echoed with his vocal fame.'[18] Turning to composition, he made his way to London, where he achieved renown as singer, composer and impresario. Although he is better known for *Tom Bowling* (based on his sailor brother, Captain Thomas Dibdin who was killed by lightning at the Cape of Good Hope), his most singular achievement was to compose the music for the first opera ever to be televised in this country: Bickerstaffe's *Padlock*.

One Winchester family that made a significant contribution to the Cathedral's musical life in the 18th century was that of the Jourds. At the beginning of the century there were no fewer than three Lay Clerks of this name, one of whom – Richard Jourd – rose to the office of Sub-Sacrist. The family evidently kept up with the musical developments of the day – at about the time of Handel's death in London one of their offspring was christened William Handel Jourd in honour of the great composer. He joined the Choir at a time when the Organist was pressing for increased forces; and in June 1772 the Chapter agreed 'that two additional choristers be provided by Mr Kent'.[19] It was not long, however, before the aged James Kent resigned – he was already in his 70s – and in the summer of 1774 he was replaced by another ex-Chorister, Peter Fussell. The new Organist had been one of the first pupils at Mr. Holloway's school and had left the Choir in 1744 to be bound apprentice for an unknown trade: ten years later he became a Lay Vicar. Peter Fussell appears to have been the first Organist to have been accorded the luxury of an assistant, rather than training his own apprentice, though he had to contribute £20 from his own annual salary towards the pay of his deputy.[20]

From 1781 our Choristers were able to earn extra pocket money by helping out in Winchester College Chapel. At that time the number of Quiristers had fallen to six – well below the statutory 16 – and they were chosen 'for their deserving circumstances rather than their singing ability'.[21] Having been ejected from College, they now lived with their parents or in lodgings in the City, and their status in Wykeham's foundation was 'little better than that of the servants whose livery they wore'.[22] It is small wonder that musical standards at the College were low. The College accounts show annual payments to Choristers from 1781 until the mid-19th century; for example, 'to four Cathedral choristers attending College chapel, one year to Whitsuntide: 2 guineas each'.[23]

From the same period come the Chapter's first attempts to regulate the attendance of the Organist, which seems to have become a matter of personal whim: perhaps the Canons regretted allowing Fussell an assistant. In November 1782 it was ordered 'that the senior Chorister do attend in the Chapter House [. . .] every 15th day, and bring an account in writing of the days when the Choristers have attended the Organist, their master, during the preceding fortnight'.[24] Such controls were to become increasingly necessary in the 19th century, under such Organists as Chard and Wesley, who were notorious for their slackness in attendance.

George William Chard, a former chorister of St Paul's Cathedral, was appointed Assistant Organist (and *de facto* Lay Vicar) in May 1791, aged twenty-six. As Peter Fussell neared the end of a long career, Chard assumed many of his duties and in 1800 was given sole responsibility for 'instructing the Choristers in singing and recommending to the Chapter proper boys for Choristers'.[25] Chard enjoyed a good reputation as a trainer of boys' voices, and it was possibly due to his influence that in 1800 a new song-school was established in the long chamber now used as the Library's 'Exhibition Room', where a harpsichord was provided to accompany the boys' practices.[26]

Peter Fussell died in 1802 and Chard succeeded him as Organist, at an increased salary of £100 *per annum*. Following established custom, he delegated his responsibility for the general education of the boys. A Mr. Denett was engaged as Schoolmaster to teach the Choristers 'Reading, Writing, Spelling and Arithmetic'.[27] As well as free schooling, each boy received 'a suit of plain clothes' every Christmas and, on leaving the Choir (unless expelled), 'a guinea a year for the time he has been in the choir' towards his apprentice fee.[28]

After an enthusiastic start, Chard's interest in the Cathedral's music seems to have waned: his attendance at Winchester College Chapel (where he was also Organist, the two posts having been held jointly since 1729) was equally infrequent. The Chapter regularly reminded him of his statutory duties, admonishing him 'to teach the boys by note'[29] and threatening him with dismissal, but Chard seems to have been increasingly absorbed by the musical and social activities in the City which led to his election as Mayor of Winchester in 1832. As we shall see, the Canons were unimpressed both by this honour and the Doctorate in Music bestowed upon their Organist by the University of Cambridge in 1812.

The Cathedral authorities were possibly more successful in establishing discipline among the Choristers and Lay Clerks. The Chapter Minutes throughout the first half of the 19th century bear witness to the Chapter's determination to enforce attendance, punctuality and respectability on the part of the Choir. Suddenly the Lay Vicars discovered to their cost that their private lives were being scrutinised: like Lay Vicar Sharp, who was 'reprimanded in the Chapter Room in front of the whole Choir' for 'admitting improper persons and lodgers into his house';[30] or Lay Vicar Simmonds, who was suspended after a three-day hangover ('illness brought on by his own misconduct')[31] and finally sacked for 'a new case of drunkenness'.[32]

As for the Choristers, they must have realised that the carefree days of the 18th century were over (during which they seem to have beguiled many a tedious hour by carving their names upon the panels of their box-like choir stalls) when, by Chapter Order, their seats in Church were raised 'so that when sitting down they may be seen by the Minor Canons and Lay Vicars'.[33] This measure was not successful in curbing the Choristers' unruly behaviour: stronger action had to be taken to show that the Chapter meant business. So at the June Chapter meeting of 1814, it was announced that the senior Chorister, James Masters, and his younger partner in crime, George Bishop, would be fined 10 shillings each for repeatedly 'flinging stones in the Church yard', and Dr. Chard was 'directed to punish them both corporally'.[34] Having thus dealt with two boys by way of example, the Choristers were publicly warned that 'any one who shall be found guilty of the same or other disorderly conduct shall be immediately expelled from the Choir'. A few months later, Chorister Seal was dismissed for 'extreme misconduct'[35] and his brother appears to have left with him, in a gesture of fraternal solidarity.

There can be little doubt that the disciplinary difficulties that faced the Chapter were largely the result of Dr. Chard's neglect of his duties as Organist. His appearances in the Cathedral seem to have been limited to Sundays and major feasts, and he ignored the statutory requirement to instruct the Choristers. In February 1815 the Chapter addressed their first Remonstrance to Dr. Chard, stating their determination 'to enforce the statutes and regulations of the Church in order to remedy the Evils which have resulted from his neglect of duties'[36] and reminding him that he would be considered responsible for all misconduct on the part of the Choristers. The senior Chorister was given the task of keeping an attendance register and making entries in a special book 'specifying the course of musical Instruction during the previous week and the attendance of the organist and deputy organist'.[37] These measures do not appear to have been effective, and at the end of 1818 another Admonition was delivered to Dr. Chard, pointing out that in the previous year he had 'attended at the singing room only 14 times, having been once absent for more than 3 months altogether'.[38]

Meanwhile, the Chapter decided to appoint a new Lay Vicar, with the title of 'Schoolmaster of the Choristers', to instruct them 'in music and singing if he be capable, but certainly in writing, reading and arithmetic, and paying careful attention to their morals and conduct'.[39] He would be permitted to take 10 non-Chorister pupils on his own account. An advertisement was inserted in the local newspapers and in 1818 William Garrett was appointed, at an annual salary of £51 and, like the 'singing-men', a 'reward' of one shilling for each attendance at Evensong, provided he had attended six morning services in the week. From William Garrett's tenure of office date the first recorded attempts at educating the Choristers and the College 'Quiristers' together, at No.5 College Street (now demolished): the experiment did not outlast the trial period of six months.[40]

In order to maintain their control over Choristers' behaviour, the Dean and Chapter demanded a weekly report from the Schoolmaster. Some of these reports survive, bound in a volume known as the *Choristers' Book*:[41] the elegant copper-plate hand of Mr. Garrett contrasts strikingly with the comments occasionally scrawled by the Canon in Residence. Indeed, Garrett's calligraphy later earned him two guineas a year, when he used to write in the words to anthems copied by the senior Choristers.

Most of the weekly reports consist of the laconic observation: 'The behaviour of the Choristers during the week has been very good'. Garrett evidently wished to show that he was master of the situation. However, the misdemeanours of the Choristers, occasionally reported, give an amusing insight into the problems that faced the Cathedral authorities. One William Dyer appears to have caused particular trouble. He frequently shirked services, encouraged, it seems, by the senior Chorister, John Bishop (younger brother of George Bishop, the stone thrower). In January 1820 the Canon in Residence enquired whether 'Dyer has behaved more attentively?'. But later that year the boy was in trouble again, missing services and, together with John Bishop, 'cracking and eating nuts during the Service'. A few weeks later, Dyer was guilty of 'gross misconduct', having obtained leave of absence under false pretences. After a further incident when four boys, including Bishop and Dyer, were involved in 'some impropriety in the distribution of the Choristers' fees', Mr. Garrett appealed to the Chapter to investigate the conduct of the senior boys. This seems to have been successful in some cases: not in that of William Dyer! His name continues to appear in the conduct book: 'Beating a Junior Boy', 'Fighting' and 'Improper Conduct' are some of his offences, and he was at the centre of a lengthy altercation between Mr. Garrett and the Chapter over the question of who should grant the Choristers leave of absence from services.

Despite these problems, Choristers at Winchester probably received a tolerable education compared to that of their counterparts at many other cathedrals. We have no record of a visitation by the formidable Miss Maria Hackett, 'the choir-boys' friend' (though perhaps regarded with less than friendly eyes by Deans and Chapters). Concerned at the poor education and general conditions of choristers, she made it her business to visit each cathedral in the country once every three years. If she did visit Winchester, she may have found our arrangements satisfactory: unlike, for example, those made for the choristers of St Paul's Cathedral, for whom Miss Hackett eventually won an hour's formal schooling a day![42]

If the Choristers' education was satisfactory by the standards of the day, the same could not be said of their singing. Even the Canons had noticed that all was not well: in their first Remonstrance to Dr. Chard, they had asked him to instruct the Choristers 'to make the responses in a decent uniform manner and not at the highest pitch of their voices as at present which resembles a Street Cry rather than a Religious Rite'.[43] The Choristers can hardly have been encouraged by the poor attendance at the services at which they sang. In October 1825 William Cobbett attended a Sunday service in Winchester Cathedral. 'There is a *dean*, and God knows how many *prebends* belonging to this immensely rich bishopric and chapter: and there were at this "service" *two or three men, and five or six boys* in white surplices, with a congregation of *fifteen women* and *four men*. Gracious God! If William of Wykham could at that moment have been raised from his tomb!'.[44]

William Garrett's position as sole schoolmaster of the Choristers was brought to an end in November 1839, when it was decided to unite the 'two Choristers schools of the Church and the College as the foundation of a training school'.[45] The training college of the 'Winchester Diocesan Training Association' had opened in August of that year, at 27 St Swithun Street, with just seven students.[46] So once again the Choristers and the College Quiristers (who continued to board at No.5 College Street) were educated together. The link between the two foundations was further strengthened in September 1841, when, continuing the help already being given to the College choir, two Choristers were permitted to attend the Quiristers' practice twice weekly.[47]

In 1841 the young William Whiting enrolled as a student of the senior section of the Training School: he boarded at 27 St Swithun Street and his name appears at that address in the 1841 Census where his age is given as fifteen.[48] He was later to achieve fame as author of the hymn *Eternal Father, Strong to Save*. His acquaintance with the Cathedral Choristers was brief: the following year, at a surprisingly young age, he took sole charge of the boarding and education of the Quiristers, at No.5 College Street.[49] It seems that the Choristers continued to receive at least part of their general education at the Training School until it removed to Wolvesey in the late 1840s.

George Chard died on 23 May 1849 and was buried in the College cloisters. Aged and infirm during his latter years, he had relied increasingly on his deputy, Benjamin Long, who conducted the weekly 'full practices' instituted in the 1840s, and compensated somewhat for the failings of his superior. Perhaps the most realistic obituary of Dr. Chard is contained in a letter which Charles Knyvett wrote to Samuel Sebastian Wesley, who had solicited his support in his application for the vacant post of Organist:

Although possessing a very nice feeling for music, [Chard] was much more attached to fly-fishing and hunting, for frequently when on his journeys to scholars, [. . .] if perchance he heard the hounds, 'Tally ho! 'tis the merry ton'd horn!' says he, [. . .] and with or without the brush of the Fox would brush into the first Public house handy for brandy, pipes and backie, till sometimes breakfast was next morning waiting his return, besides the many pupils that had been hard practising . . .'[50]

Wesley's application was successful but, before he was admitted, the Dean and Chapter delivered to him an *Explanation of the Statutes of the Cathedral affecting the Organist, and amount of the Duties and conduct required of him.*[51] He was reminded that, according to the Statutes relating to the Organist, 'if he be negligent or insolent in teaching, he is to be put out of office after being thrice warned'. As to the education of the Choristers, it was made clear that Wesley was to give them 'the benefit of his personal instruction in Music and Singing, and [be] responsible [. . .] for their progress and improvement'. Having thus protected their interests as best they could, the Dean and Chapter admitted Samuel Sebastian Wesley as Organist and Master of the Choristers on 5 October 1849, at an annual salary of £150.[52]

Dr. Wesley's arrival in Winchester roughly coincided with the 19th-century revival of interest in church music in this country, after 150 years of neglect. He played an outstanding part in this revival himself, of course; and other factors include the Oxford Movement, the efforts of Miss Maria Hackett and, perhaps, the new availability of cheap printed music. In 1852 a Royal Commission was set up 'to enquire into the state and condition of the cathedral and collegiate churches of England and Wales'.[53] Wesley was never one to be brief. His reply to the commissioners' questions on music at Winchester runs to more than 5,000 words! He included a scheme which shows in considerable detail his conception of the organist's rôle; and incidentally reveals a social bias which might raise an eyebrow or two today.

'A Cathedral Choir', he maintained, 'should consist of at least twelve lay singers and ten to twelve boys'. The Lay Clerks should preferably not be tradesmen: 'A good tradesman is almost sure to be a bad singer and vice versa. On enquiry it will probably be found that at least half the number of choir men engaged in trade had once or oftener been bankrupt'. The boys, likewise, should be 'of some refinement', from a 'comfortable home', and should not be drawn from 'the lowest grade [. . .] which renders all delicacy of utterance an impossibility'. The choristers should be educated at a special school, whose principal might be a musician: the school could be self-supporting, by giving 'frequent concerts, at rates of admission available to the working classes'. One might well ask whether the working classes would have much interest in the school from which they were so categorically excluded.

Some of Dr. Wesley's ideals were achieved at Winchester during his period of office. The number of Choristers rose to 12 at the end of 1857; and although the commissioners' questionnaire addressed to 'The Rev. the Master of the Cathedral School' was returned by the Chapter Clerk with the observation 'there is no such person',[54] five years after the enquiry the boys were all educated (and many of them boarded) in the same establishment. Finally, Wesley's rather obvious judgement on organs, 'the bad cathedral organs should be replaced by good ones', seems to have been heeded: in 1854 he persuaded the Dean and Chapter to buy two-thirds of the huge instrument built by 'Father' Willis for the Great Exhibition, which he must have admired when it was housed in the Crystal Palace in Hyde Park. No doubt he would have bought the complete organ had there been room for it; but in the event the remaining third was shipped to America. This mighty instrument was one of the largest organs ever made in this country, and the first to be equipped with combination pistons.

Some years earlier, in 1847, the Training School had moved from St Swithun Street to Wolvesey Palace, by kind permission of the Bishop, who lived at Farnham Castle in those days. The School remained there until shortly after 1858, when, as a result of an adverse report on the sanitary conditions of the building, new premises were planned on healthy West Hill: the present King Alfred's College. During the Wolvesey days, one of the senior lecturers – a Mr. Sheppard – formed a Mathematical and Commercial School, and in 1852 this broke away from the parent institution, moving first into No.3 St Swithun Street and, two years later, into neighbouring Canon Street. When Mr. Garrett retired from full-time school-mastering in 1856 it was decided that the Choristers should attend Mr. Sheppard's Commercial School as boarders, the Chapter paying half the fees.

This arrangement began in January 1857. The Chapter devised a list of *Arrangements relative to Mr Garrett*,[55] whose duties now consisted in little more than accompanying the Choristers to and from the school, inserting markers in the Lay Vicars' singing books before each service, supervising the Cathedral Library and looking after the Churchyard and the common stables. Now that boarding places were available, it was possible to entice Choristers from outside Winchester; and in January 1857 notice was given in the local newspapers of the forthcoming election of three Choristers 'from any locality provided they have a voice and ear for music'.[56]

However, just when the foundations seemed laid for improvement in the Choir's musical standards, Wesley had his first serious brush with the Chapter. Indeed, it seems surprising that a man of Samuel Sebastian's unshakeable convictions should not have clashed with his employers earlier. In spite of all Dr. Wesley's high-flown phrases about choir schools and choristers' education, he appears to have been as indolent as his predecessors when it came to instructing his own singing-boys. In November 1858 the Canons agreed it was 'essential [. . .] that the Instruction of the Choristers in the Rudiments of Musical services and in the practice of singing should be more effectively secured'.[57] Wesley does not seem to have responded to this implied criticism of his professional abilities. A year later, the Chapter did some sums and pointed out to Dr. Wesley that since the previous November he had attended less than half the possible number of services: it was 'their painful duty' to present the Organist with the first of the three admonitions prescribed by Statute. Not only had Dr. Wesley been absent on 383 occasions, but he had frequently left the Cathedral Organ to the care of 'a lad of only 14 years of age'. The Canons observed that only two of the Choristers were competent to sing solos: the Organist and Master of the Choristers had failed in his duty to train the boys to sing. Finally, they complained of his lack of 'respectful and courteous attention to the wishes of the Dean and Chapter'.[58]

Wesley's reaction to this criticism is unrecorded. In March 1860 the former Muniment Room in the South Transept was converted into a practice room for the boys, but the result seems to have been to make the Canons even more aware of the poor behaviour of their Choristers. At their General Chapter meeting in November they forbade the boys to 'leave the singing school for Recreation prior to the commencement of morning Service', and took the opportunity of pointing out to the Organist that 'the Choristers' school is in an unsatisfactory state'.[59]

Matters came to a head again in September 1861, when Wesley received a second formal admonition from the Dean and Chapter. He had neglected to attend choir practices, with disastrous results on at least two occasions; and when the Vice Dean and Canon in Residence had finally managed to persuade him to attend a voice trial for a potential Lay Vicar, he had first refused to give his opinion and then replied that 'even if I were in favour of this candidate, it probably wouldn't do him any good. Of course I should give my opinion if I thought it would be acted upon in a just and straightforward manner!'[60]

Wesley appears to have avoided his third and final admonition, but many other complaints were to be levelled against him in the Chapter Room before he left for Gloucester in 1865. The Dean and Chapter must have breathed a sigh of relief. Nevertheless, Winchester had undoubtedly gained from its brief acquaintance with one of the foremost figures in 19th-century English church music, despite his personal shortcomings and difficult temper.

In February 1865, Dr. Arnold was 'unanimously' appointed Organist in succession to Samuel Sebastian Wesley, though it appears from the Chapter Book that only Dean Garnier was present at this private 'Chapter meeting'.[61] At his installation, the Canons took the precaution of reading to the new Organist the *Explanation of the Statutes and Rules* that they had formulated for Dr. Wesley, 16 years previously.[62]

The following year the Choristers moved house once more. Now that the Training School had removed to West Hill, Wolvesey Palace was available for occupation, and Mr. Sheppard installed his Diocesan Commercial School in the larger premises. He described the facilities in glowing terms in an advertisement composed for the *Hampshire Chronicle*: 'The House is admirably adapted for its present use and is replete with every convenience for the comfort of its inmates. The extensive grounds, in addition to the spacious Gardens, contain an inclosed Meadow for the recreation of the Pupils'.[63]

Mr. Garrett seems to have found walking to and from Wolvesey too demanding, and he retired from his long-held post as Master in charge of the Choristers in 1869. A Mr. Somersford replaced him for a short time;[64] then a well-known Winchester musical figure, William Pimlott,[65] self-styled 'professor of singing', who ran the 'Vocal Lyceum' in Eastgate Street.[66] As a boy he had been a chorister at Romsey Abbey, and for rather more than 30 years he was Winchester Cathedral's bass soloist and Lay Clerk in charge of the pitch-pipe. William Garrett continued to mind the Cathedral Library until the end of 1873 when he was awarded an annual pension of £100 'in consequence of his long and faithful services'.[67]

In June 1871 the Canons reconsidered the arrangements for their Choristers' education. All was not well at Wolvesey, 'the parents complaining of things in the School and dissatisfied, and many of them long delaying their payments – and further, it was found that the Choristers' term of duty in the Cathedral and practising could not but very materially interfere with the general work of the School'.[68] It was decided that an empty house in the Close, No.4 (now the Judges' Lodgings), should be used as a day-school for the Choristers. Thus from January 1872 the boys lived with their parents in the town, receiving their clothing, books and education at No.4 free of charge. Their number was increased to 14: the six Foundation Boys prescribed by Statute, and eight other 'Probationers, to be put on the Foundation as vacancies occurred'.[69] A young Lay Vicar, William Southcott, was appointed Schoolmaster of the Choristers at an annual stipend of £50

I Winchester Cathedral Choristers in 1877, six years after the opening of the Choir School at No. 4, The Close. Back row: (*left to right*) E.A. Bailey, H.F. Webb, C.B. Cross, E.W. Savage, E. Deavin; front row: R. Jupe, W.S. Taplin, F.T. Bowen, F. Hardy, W.J. Beckett, W.H. Pimlott, S.G. Corps, E.C. Young

II Winchester Cathedral Choir, Christmas 1913. Adults (*left to right*), back row: Archie Clements, Sheepwash, Jabez Whitwam, Virger Elkins, Major, Edward Hone; seated: William Southcott, Dr. Prendergast, Precentor Wickham, Dean Furneaux, Minor-Canon Slater, Minor-Canon Walton, Herbert Elsmore

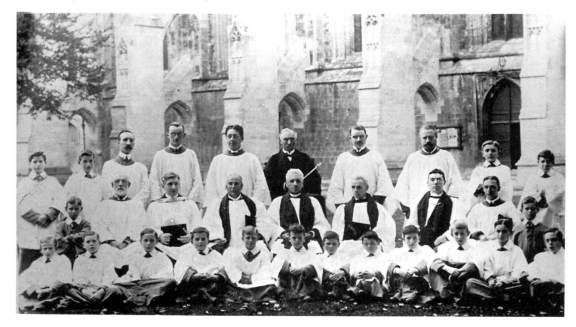

and rent-free accommodation at the school.[70] In addition, he was permitted to teach a dozen or so prospective Choristers from the town, charging their parents £1 per quarter.

Six years later the Choristers were joined by 16 temporary pupils: the Quiristers of Winchester College. These had found themselves without a Schoolmaster on the death of William Whiting in May 1878, and although his daughter Mary taught them for a few months, it was clear that this could be only a temporary expedient. The College authorities applied to the Dean and Chapter for permission for the Quiristers to attend classes at No.4 The Close. The Chapter 'agreed that permission be given as an experiment to commence Sept 19th for one year – each party being at liberty to terminate this agreement at Xmas 1878'.[71]

The arrangement was not a success: 'It was soon found to be very inconvenient and undesirable. There was a divided government, each set of boys being under its own Master, and a good deal of jealousy between the two sets of boys was apparent.'[72] Thus the experiment of educating Choristers and Quiristers under the same roof was short-lived: it was exactly 100 years before the Quiristers were permanently incorporated into the Chapter's Pilgrims' School in 1978. Meanwhile the Headmaster of the College, conscious that the lease of Cheyney Court (where the Quiristers then boarded) was to expire in 1882, decided to build a new house at 64 Kingsgate Street to serve as the Quiristers' School.

William Southcott appears to have been a strict schoolmaster: too strict for the parents of Chorister Harry Twyman, who asked for their son to be removed from the school 'on the ground of his not being happy or comfortable with Mr and Mrs Southcott'.[73] He boarded instead with Mr. Newnham of the Hyde Dairy.

A letter survives, written by a young Chorister, Henry Edward Holloway, at the very start of his summer holidays, on 2 July 1884. 'Mr Southcott hopes that you will do all you can to enable me to get up my home lessons thoroughly because we have not so much time for study during the day as other schools have, and he will then be spared the pain of inflicting punishment'.[74] The entire letter is far too good to be true and was evidently written under the Master's dictation!

An acquaintance of the late Canon Goodman sent him some memories of life at No.4.

The House was in a very delapidated condition, the interior being distinctly unattractive. A glass of milk and a bun was served out to each boy every morning. A Miss Jacob [Miss Edith Sophia Jacob, daughter of Archdeacon Philip Jacob] took a deep interest in the school, and her Bible Class was a regular feature. The education in comparison with present-day standards could be described as 'homely'; but the school turned out a long sequence of successes in after-life, both in other callings and in the musical profession. The choir during this period was strong vocally, solo boys of very good calibre being a marked feature, supported by day-boys from the City.[75]

In 1887, Mr. Southcott and the Organist came to blows: in an unguarded moment, the Schoolmaster had criticised the procedure of Dr. Arnold and the Precentor at the voice trials. He was reprimanded, but appears to have struck back and lost the ensuing battle. His 'charges against the Precentor and the Organist' were considered unjust and he was requested to 'resign his position as schoolmaster'.[76]

Mr. Southcott remained on the Cathedral pay-roll as a Lay Clerk until 1916, but his position as Schoolmaster of the Choristers was taken by Mr. Edward Hone, who moved into No.4 with his wife and young family in 1887.

There were now 16 Choristers, and their remuneration was complex. Six of them counted as Foundation Boys under the Caroline Statutes, of whom the two seniors received £4 *per annum* as 'foundation money' and the four juniors £2. The other 10 Choristers were eligible for four Boarding Scholarships to the value of £24 a year. Four boys were to be trained as Solo Boys and later received an additional stipend for this distinction. Finally, there were from four to eight Probationers in the school, to fill the vacancies among the Choristers as they occurred.[77]

The Hones were to spend only a short time in the Close. In December 1894, the Barracks – the only completed wing of Wren's famous King's House – was destroyed by fire. As a result, the Hampshire Regiment moved to Serles House in Southgate Street, which had formerly been used as accommodation for Her Majesty's Judges when on the Western Circuit.[78] The County Council looked for suitable premises in Winchester to replace these Judges' Lodgings and eventually agreed with the Chapter to rent No.4 The Close, on a 999-year lease.[79] A house just outside the Close in Colebrook Street, Colebrook House, was purchased for £1,500 to serve as the new Choristers' School, and by 1897 the building was ready for occupation.[80]

Chapter Three

COLEBROOK HOUSE

COLEBROOK HOUSE, a large 16th-century building, remodelled in the reign of Queen Anne, provided Edward Hone with considerable space for his large family, the Choristers, and a number of 'Private Boarders'. It had been twice used as a girls' boarding school in the early 19th century, and although the lay-out of the building precluded any rigid separation of the school and the 'private' side, there was nevertheless a distinct contrast between the elegant rooms at the front of the building, facing the east end of the Cathedral, and south over the Close, and the domestic wing on the north and east sides of the house, which had long, uneven corridors and unlikely flights of stairs. The garden was particularly attractive, with its Mill Stream emerging from underneath the east wing of the house, and a smaller tributary, formed perhaps by Ethelwold in the 10th century when he brought 'sweet streams of fishful water' to cleanse the Old and New Minsters.

A complex salary scale was devised whereby Mr. Hone would receive £15 for each Chorister and £50 as a Housemaster's allowance; the allowance was to be reduced by £5 for every non-Chorister boarder he received over the number of ten. This arrangement proved most unsatisfactory and money was in short supply in the Hone household, particularly during the War years.

One of the earliest pupils at Colebrook House was Philip Sawyer. At the age of seven, he was boarding at Miss Wells' school in Southgate Street. One Sunday, whilst out walking, they met Minor-Canon Marshall, the Precentor. 'And who is the boy?', he enquired. Miss Wells explained, and he suggested 'Take him to the Cathedral tomorrow at 9.00 a.m. and Dr. Arnold will try his voice'. As Philip Sawyer later recalled: 'The upshot was that I was accepted and became a pro-bationer chorister. I wrote to my mother the same day. I still have that letter. It is dated Monday, May 14th 1900'.

Among the Choristers singing in the Choir at that time were two of Mr. Hone's five sons: Percival and Reginald. Four of the Hone boys were to become Choristers, and in 1901 Edward Hone himself was elected a full Lay Clerk, having been a 'supernumerary tenor' for a few years.

Hardly had Philip Sawyer been dubbed a Chorister than he sang at the Millen-nary Celebrations of King Alfred, in 1901, when the famous statue was set up at

23

the end of the Broadway. Dr. Arnold composed a special anthem for the occasion; and there was a festival service in the Cathedral, during which the combined choirs of Winchester, Chichester and Salisbury, together with the choir of the Chapel Royal, sang Wesley's great anthem *Ascribe unto the Lord* and other suitable musical offerings. This proved to be George Arnold's last major undertaking; he fell ill that winter and died in January 1902, only four days after his forthcoming resignation had been announced. As a musician, he was fated to be over-shadowed by his former teacher and predecessor, S. S. Wesley; but he will be remembered at Winchester as the man who established the Diocesan Choral Festival, whereby parish choirs periodically invaded Winchester in train-loads, to sing in the Nave of our great Cathedral.

Philip Sawyer remembers Dr. Arnold as a frightening and not altogether likeable character, and preferred his successor, William Prendergast (a former pupil of Arnold's), who moved to Winchester from St Paul's Church, Edinburgh, at a starting salary of £250 *per annum* and rent-free accommodation at No.5 The Close.

It seems to have been largely on Dr. Prendergast's advice that Colebrook House was made an all-boarding school in 1905. Existing dayboys became boarders, and Mr. Hone's allowance was increased considerably. Further dormitories were created and shortly afterwards a new classroom block was planned.

This building, completed in 1908, is of some interest in view of its subsequent history. It consisted of two large classrooms under a high, tunnel-vaulted roof, lit by a window at either end. Between the classrooms was a sliding partition that could be closed when teaching was going on; by opening the partition, a much larger space was created for recreation, Christmas parties and the like. When in 1925 the Choir School was re-established in the Close, at No.9, this building was laboriously dismantled and re-erected on the south side of Dome Alley. Little changed, except that electric light replaced the old gas lighting. The classrooms were used by The Pilgrims' School until 1963 when the building was converted into two small cottages for the Cathedral staff.

Towards the end of Philip Sawyer's time at Colebrook House, Edward Hone obtained an assistant, Percy J. Spillett. The two men ran the school from 1905 until Edward Hone left Winchester in 1922. Both equally memorable in their own ways, they left an indelible impression on the minds of the Choristers they educated.

Although so totally different in temper and physique, they seemed to have formed an ideal team. 'Teddy' Hone was a heavily-built, bearded man, not unlike his namesake Edward VII in appearance. He was somewhat vain, and towards the end of the War a newly-discovered secret amused the boys: 'Teddy' dyed his beard! But their Headmaster was one to be treated with the greatest respect: the boys lived in constant fear of him, and the school *régime* was severe. Indeed, when one boy who had fallen foul of him ran away, the cry that went up was one of 'Nutt has escaped!' 'Teddy' Hone was a strict disciplinarian and the cane which he kept in a roll-top desk in the schoolroom was in fairly constant use. 'Many were the bashings on the head and slashes on the (left) hand I had from him', recalls one former Chorister, 'but he had a kindlier side, and later, as I grew older, we were on better terms'.

'Teddy' was a good teacher of English, particularly grammar. He also took certain boys for piano lessons in the evenings, boxing their ears unsparingly when

III The schoolroom, Colebrook House

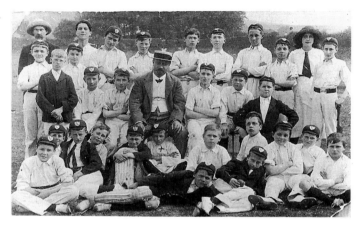

IV Colebrook House cricketers, c.1915. Choristers include Eric Greene (front left). Back row: 'Spilly' and Marjorie Hone. Seated: 'Teddy' Hone

V School group in the garden of Colebrook House, c.1918

wrong notes were played. He had a good tenor voice, and occasionally sang solos in the Cathedral. One such solo contained the words 'for I am a worm and no man', after which 'Teddy' would always joke, 'Well, if I am a worm, I'm a pretty fat one!'

While 'Teddy' Hone was severe, irascible and feared, his assistant, 'Spilly', was mild and sympathetic. He was a bachelor, tall, thin and bespectacled, with a drooping moustache, scholarly in his mannerisms, and walked with a slight stoop which belied his sporting ability. He looked after the junior section of the school and was particularly popular with the younger boys.

'He was a magician', wrote Frank Baker, who later made 'Spilly' the subject of a novel, *Sweet Chariot*, published by Eyre & Spottiswoode in 1942. 'He was the man who opened the doors of literature to me. We ragged him unmercifully, I'm afraid.'

'Spilly' seldom lost his temper. However Frank Baker recalls an occasion when 'I once behaved outrageously to Mrs. Tyler, Teddy Hone's grim old sister, when Teddy was away for the day, and Spilly gave me the thrashing of a lifetime. Days later, he said, "I think we agree to forget what happened, Baker?". I eagerly agreed.'

'By then I was almost boss of the odd little School, and agreed with Spilly that smoking must be stopped with the smaller boys. I myself continued to smoke Russian cigarettes, and Spilly winked at it.'

Indeed, 'Spilly' certainly knew much more about the 'unofficial' side of school life than the Headmaster. Occasionally he would make this clear, prefacing his comment with the words, 'I suggest . . .' and a sucking of the upper lip which made a sound like 'tchch'.

Percy Spillett was an authority on palaeolithic implements. He had an impressive collection of artefacts and during Sunday walks with the boys would examine the spoil from rabbit-holes in the hope of finding an arrow-head. 'Those wonderful Sunday walks to St Catherine's Hill', recalls Frank Baker, 'the ins and blocked outs of the Maze, the stones we found and offered to Spilly hoping they were prehistoric treasures – they hardly ever were.'

If an arrow-head was unearthed, 'Spilly' would sometimes bind it to a stick in resemblance of the real thing; Choristers were sent to the City Museum with really interesting discoveries.

Before one of these Sunday walks, Chorister Jimmy Burchell 'borrowed' a stone implement from a box-full that Percy Spillett kept in the school boot-room. 'On the Downs, I went up to him and pretended that I had just found the arrow-head'. His reply was characteristic: 'I suggest . . . tchch! . . . that you put that back where you *really* found it!'

The daily life of Choristers at Colebrook House lies well within living memory, and although the reminiscences from which this account is compiled span a period of more than 20 years, including a World War, the routine of school life appears to have changed little during that time. From 1903 until 1919 the boys knew the same Dean, Organist, Headmaster and assistant master; and this unchanging team assured continuity.

The bell rang at 7 o'clock in the morning, winter and summer, and the boys unwillingly washed in cold water. One of the dormitories (named 'Coppins' after a previous tenant) had its own wash-basins: the Chapter had installed wash-rooms for the boys near to the other bedrooms. Breakfast was at 8 o'clock: thick slices of bread and dripping (butter in more affluent times) known as 'toke', an Anglo-Saxon term, it seems. This plain fare was enlivened with fish paste or marmalade. After the War, 'toke' was replaced by toast for breakfast, and the duty boys who prepared it were rewarded with crusts: a much sought-after privilege! Cooked breakfasts were unknown, except on the morning of the school holidays, when the boys were sent home fortified by a boiled egg.

Wearing their Eton suits, mortar-boards and carefully-blackened boots ('We weren't allowed shoes and boots had to be blacked front and back'), the Choristers made their way in a 'crocodile' to the practice room in the South Transept for an hour's rehearsal. The small two-manual practice room organ (now in Weston Church on Southampton Water) was hand-blown; and miscreants were set to pump, encouraged by 'Billy' Prendergast's cries of 'Blow boy, blow!'. Should the supply of air fail, the organ would wheeze to silence, and 'Billy' would exclaim 'That boy deserves a whipping'; but he never carried out his jocular threat.

At 9.45 the Lay Clerks began to arrive. Ignoring Dr. Wesley's warnings of imminent bankruptcy, many of them owned a business in the town: like Jabez Whitwam, with his music shop, or the alto Archie Clements, who ran a photographic business and took many pictures of the choir. Mattins lasted for just three quarters of an hour and was followed by morning school until one o'clock. Then lunch: 'A two-course affair, and I would call it tolerable'. All meals were taken in the elegant dining room at the back of the house: 'Teddy' carved, and his wife and daughters handed round the vegetables. During the War years, Marjorie and Dorothy Hone acted as Matrons, when not on Red Cross duty. H. E. ('Peter') Day still recalls Dorothy Hone's anguished cry of 'mind the plates, boys!' when plates were scraped.

The afternoon arrangements were flexible, depending mainly on the weather. Lunch was normally followed by afternoon school until 3.45; but if the weather was fine, lessons might be postponed until the evening, and games played instead – cricket or football, depending on the time of year. In any case, Evensong followed at 4 o'clock. There was then a further practice for the boys until tea-time: they were joined by the Lay Clerks for a full rehearsal on Mondays and Saturdays.

Arrangements for Wednesday afternoon were rather different: being 'plain day', there was no Evensong or practice, and the afternoon was spent playing games or going for long archaeological rambles, which 'Spilly', with his wide knowledge of a number of subjects, 'made really interesting'. Similarly, on Saturday afternoons there were no lessons; but the boys had to return from their games, walk or (in post-War years) shopping in time for Evensong.

Tea, at about 6 o'clock was 'a miserable affair'. It consisted of tea and 'toke', with black treacle which had inevitably spread all over the dish on which it was served, before the boys arrived. Things looked up slightly on Saturdays, when jam was provided. Sundays were better still, with cake, and the likelihood of an invitation to tea in the Close, perhaps with Mrs. Sumner at No.1, founder of the Mothers' Union and still an exquisite pianist at the age of 90, or with Dean Furneaux, who regularly had six Choristers to tea each Sunday. After tea, the remaining Choristers would join the party, all would settle in the Long Gallery, and the Dean's daughter would read them an exciting novel, in serial form.

Most boys supplemented the school's basic provender with food from tuck-boxes, or parcels sent from home. One enterprising Chorister ran a lucrative business, collecting 'investments' from willing boys at the beginning of term, buying jam, and selling it to the others at tea-time: profits were distributed among the shareholders.

After tea there were further lessons, if these had not taken place during the afternoon, or an opportunity for piano practice or a lesson with Mr. Hone in the tiny music rooms adjoining the classroom block. Others would read or play chess in the classrooms which constituted the only playroom available to them. During the long summer evenings, they were allowed to make their way to the ruins of Wolvesey Castle (there was a short-cut from the garden of Colebrook House), a fine place for games, and the recognised *rendez-vous* for settling scores!

Before the boys went to bed at about 9 o'clock, the Matrons or one of the Hone girls would bring a dish of 'toke' and a jug of cocoa to the schoolroom; this supper could be considerably improved by toasting the underside of the bread on the coke stoves. After their supper, the boys would retire to the dormitories: there were five of these, housing about seven boys each. On the first floor was the 'Infants' dormitory for the youngest boys and the two rooms known as 'Coppins'. 'Inner Coppins was the most popular as we could hear old Spillett before he came in.' On the second floor were the dormitories called 'Saints' (a reference to Psalm 149 v. 5: 'Let the saints be joyful with glory: let them rejoice in their beds') and 'Clink' (probably after the Bishop of Winchester's ancient prison at Southwark). Spillett had a room between these dormitories, and was usually responsible for 'doing the rounds' and turning off the gas at 'lights-out'.

Sunday was a busy day for the Choristers, particularly for those who were to sing verses that day. After a later breakfast than usual, the 'verse boys' would go to Dr. Prendergast's house in the Close for a special practice. Two of them would then be dispatched to the Buttercross to buy 'Billy's' Sunday newspaper. Meanwhile, Percy Spillett would lead the 'non-versites' on a walk across that part of the water-meadows known as the 'Garden of Eden' to St Cross and back, before 11 o'clock Mattins. From about 1917, this was occasionally followed by a Choral Communion, but it would be several years before this was a regular Sunday morning service in Winchester Cathedral.

After lunch – always a cold meal – the Choristers would write letters home, or climb to the top of the Cathedral tower, before Evensong at 3.30. This was the most important of the Sunday services, and included a lengthy anthem: 'sometimes as many as twenty-eight pages!'.

There can be little doubt that the Choristers' musical commitments during the week put them at a grave disadvantage from an educational point of view. As we have seen, there were just two 'divisions' and, at times, there might be as many as 20 boys in each form. The school reports of the time show that the boys studied 'Religious Knowledge', 'Mathematics', 'English Subjects', 'Languages' and 'Drawing'; but although Messrs. Hone and Spillett taught competently, time was not available to study these subjects in great depth. Roy Cuthbert recalls that when it was suggested that he might enter Winchester College, a special entrance paper had to be set, to make up for the subjects he had missed. He was at an advantage in 'Religious Knowledge' however: being blessed with an exceptional memory, he had learned 'large sections of the Book of Common Prayer and the Bible by heart'. At regular intervals, clerics would descend on the school to examine the boys in Scripture. Spillett would put young Cuthbert in a prominent position where he was likely to catch the examiner's eye. 'As soon as the question was asked, I was expected to put up my hand and shout "sir! . . . sir!"'. The scheme always worked, and the poor boy who was expected to answer was ignored.' Thus the examiner left with an excellent impression of the boys' prowess in the Scriptures, taught by Precentor Wickham on Saturday mornings, with the help of Dorothy Hone, who held confirmation classes in the attic rooms at Colebrook known as the 'mountain top'.

In spite of the difficulties caused by the demands of the Cathedral, 'Teddy' Hone tried to create as normal a preparatory school atmosphere as possible. There was a school uniform: Eton suits in the winter, and grey flannel suits in the summer months; and, for cricket, a blazer with a badge displaying the Cathedral arms and the letters *Sch. Cath. Winton.* in purple on a white background. There was a similar badge on the purple school cap, which was replaced by a straw boater during the summer months. There was even an Old Choristers' blazer in the same colours but this had hurriedly to be changed when it was discovered to be an exact replica of the King's College Cambridge blazer!

Under the guidance of Percy Spillett, organised sport assumed the prominent place it occupies in the life of the modern prep-school boy. Soccer and cricket were played on the meadow in front of Wolvesey Palace, prepared with loving care by 'Spilly' and his team of boys, using push-mower and roller. There were tennis courts to the north of Wolvesey Castle, next to the path leading from the school to the cricket pitch, and one tennis court within the castle walls itself. The boys were taken to the City Council's Bull Drove Baths in the Itchen twice a week.

Percy Spillett was a good cricketer, a fair batsman and fine fast bowler: 'he taught many a boy how to flight the ball'. He was a patient coach, with two or three county cricketers to his credit. The Colebrook team achieved considerable success in matches against West Downs, Winton House, Peter Symonds' School and the College Quiristers. There were two annual sporting fixtures against a preparatory school at Barton-on-Sea, whither the entire school was transported in a charabanc drawn by four horses.

Not all the Choristers shared Percy Spillett's enthusiasm for cricket, as Roy Cuthbert recalls. 'On some frightful occasions, we were taken to the County Ground where terrifying adults would bowl at us as fast as they could. I went to enormous lengths to miss this outing, and on one occasion I was discovered hiding in the castle ruins. The following day, Teddy opened his roll-top desk and out came the cane. This has put me off cricket for life!'

The exceptionally cold winter of 1917 provided a change from the normal sporting pattern. There were frequent trips to Winnall Moor, where the ponds had frozen over: the boys became proficient skaters, and created their own private rink at Colebrook House by flooding the tiny playground, known as the 'Cage', with water from the stream. Normally this diminutive yard between the classroom block and the Water Gate was used as a football pitch, or a place where cricket strokes could be practised using a special extra-narrow bat.

Birds-nesting was another favourite activity, though not condoned by the adults.

VI Summer 1918. A picnic in the ruins of Wolvesey Palace. Seated at the table: Dorothy Hone, Mr and Mrs Hone, Percy Spillett

VII Colebrook House boys bathing in the Itchen at the 'Bull Drove' swimming baths

'Teddy's' grandson, Edward Hone, a probationer Chorister, recalls being stuck up a tree for several hours when his grandfather settled himself in a deck-chair beneath it to watch a cricket match! Another Chorister, Leslie Rugg, brought several kestrel eggs back from the Cathedral tower, concealed in his boater: he reckoned without the malice of his fellow-Choristers, who pulled the straw hat down over his ears. Fishing was a more legal pastime; though perhaps not the setting of night-lines out of the boot-room window into the mill-stream below. 'Teddy's' youngest son, Dudley, used to set elaborate eel-traps, and one day, at breakfast-time, was found to have caught a shiny black cycle inner-tube, thoughtfully hooked on by his fellows!

Other boys followed more studious pursuits, photography for instance. 'Spilly' helped them set up a darkroom in the attic of Colebrook House. Obtaining supplies of film, paper and chemicals proved a problem for a time, until the boys discovered a benefactor, one Captain Phelps, who had a financial interest in the Hampshire Brewery. The routine was unsophisticated.

'Afternoon, Captain Phelps!'

'Afternoon, m'boy, afternoon; how are you? Anything you want?'

And off they would go to Wride the Chemist, in Jewry Street. Spillett came to hear of this 'arrangement' but it is not recorded that he discouraged it.

Food occupies a prominent place in the memories of old Choristers. This is probably largely explained by the fact that many contributors to this account were at Colebrook House during the War, when provisions were scarce. 'Teddy' Hone's daughter-in-law found Mrs. Hone weeping in the serving-room on more than one occasion because 'there wasn't enough food for the boys'. The situation improved somewhat after rationing was introduced, but it was a difficult period.

Roy Cuthbert recalls one way of supplementing the official diet. 'A narrow passage ran from Colebrook Street to the High Street; and opposite the Guildhall there was a cooked meat shop whose speciality was Saveloy sausages. The journey there was made more hazardous by the fact that the local Chief Constable lived in Abbey Passage; as his son attended Colebrook House for two terms only, we were convinced that he tipped off his father. I was once caught by Spillett, who confiscated the entire stock of sausages subscribed to by the inmates of Coppins. I do not remember how many lines he gave me!

'Even more popular than sausages were Hot Faggots and Peas from a shop in Chesil Street: a long and dangerous journey via Wharf Hill. The main problem was to borrow a basin from a girl who did the washing up in the Kitchen; furthermore, an Eton suit was not the best disguise, and both the High Street and Chesil Street were Out of Bounds.'

After the War, because of increased numbers, three boys were lodged in Abbey Passage: most conveniently situated for such forays. But Frank Faulkner and his fellows were caught eating a bag of chips in their attic lodgings by 'Teddy' Hone himself. 'I'm surprised at you, Faulkner' was his comment; and the next day, the luckless boys learned that their food had been thrown to the chickens.

An equally unofficial arrangement was instituted by the caretaker of Wolvesey Palace and his wife (for in those days, the Bishop was still residing more or less permanently at Farnham): they opened a tuck-shop in the Palace kitchen!

The boys' health was supervised by two matrons, including Dorothy Hone during the War, when it was difficult to recruit staff. Their methods were simple but effective: if a boy seemed off his food, he would be taken to the servery where two large Winchester quart bottles stood on the window-sill, one containing the 'White Medicine', the other the 'Brown Medicine'. The Matrons also supervised the Hot Bath rota: 'one hot bath a week, but if one was a crank, one could have a cold bath each day, taken in an old-fashioned hip bath'.

The Revd. Arthur Collins recollects another health problem: 'Owing to war-time restrictions we had very few sweets; but there was a delicacy known as a locust bean – evidently the same kind of "locust" which John Baptist used for food. It had a sweetish taste and, I gather, could be indigestible. Anyway, at one time there was an outbreak of appendicitis among us, and the surgeon was of the opinion that these beans could be the cause. After two or three boys had been rushed to hospital, we were forbidden to buy any more – and the War became more austere for us.'

The daily life of the Choristers was increasingly affected as the Great War continued. Patriotism was high amongst the boys: as their voices broke, some of the older Choristers added a year or two to their age in the hope of being enlisted and one, Reg Titt, managed to join the Navy as a Midshipman, though well under age. Normally, parents put an end to such attempts. The older Hone boys were now in the Army and occasionally returned to Colebrook House in uniform; the Hone daughters joined the Red Cross.

One popular walk during those years was along the Petersfield Road to Morne Hill Camp, 'a sea of mud', to watch the troops practising trenching. It was a transit camp, and at night the streets of Winchester resounded to the tramp of feet and clatter of wheels as the soldiers in full kit marched to Southampton with their horse-drawn gun carriages and heavy equipment, bound for France.

Memorial services for those killed in the War became increasingly frequent, and from 1915 the Choristers were involved in another regular Sunday commitment, the 'Soldiers' Service'.

The Lay Clerks were not particularly keen to devote any more of their time to Cathedral worship on Sundays, and a 'voluntary choir' was instituted, supported by just half the Choristers: *Decani* one week, *Cantoris* the next. The service was unambitious musically – no anthem, just chants and hymns – but it is of interest as the first regular service to be held in the Nave of the Cathedral, all other services taking place in the Quire before that date. Indeed, at the beginning of the century, the Nave was little more than a museum: dirty, ill-lit, with chairs stacked high in the chantry chapels.

Arthur Collins describes the services: 'I shall never forget the sight of the Nave full of khaki figures; often the aisles as well – although most of the aisles were occupied by recumbent figures asleep either on the benches or on the stone floor, lying in their great-coats. Nor shall I ever forget the smell of stale sweat and the peculiar smell of khaki uniforms which pervaded the Cathedral at those times. The sound of the soldiers singing their favourite hymns such as *Onward, Christian Soldiers* and *O God, our help in ages past* was really memorable. The whole Nave seemed full of the sound of men's voices, and even when Dr. Prendergast used the open diapason stops, these could not drown the noise of the singing.' So popular were these services, even among Winchester's civilian population, that they continued for many years after the Great War, as the 'Parish Evensong'.

The effects of the War became gradually more pronounced. Boys were encouraged to grow potatoes to overcome the food shortage. Black-out regulations came into force, but 'there was only one Zep raid on Winchester, and nothing happened'. The Choristers followed the progress of the War. 'One of my most vivid memories is hearing the distant rumble of sound on a June morning in 1917, and feeling the ground shake under us as our engineers blew up the Messines Ridge in the Ypres salient.'

Jimmy Burchell was Head Chorister at the time of the Armistice. 'An American officer appeared in the South Transept after Mattins and asked to see the Dean. We "hung around" and before long we learned that an armistice was to be signed and that there would be a special Evensong that day.'

A few days later, there was a special service. 'This was to be held on the dais, and "Billy" Prendergast told me that he was worried about space in which to fit all the visiting clergy who wanted to be present. I was surprised to see that space had been allocated to the Probationers and suggested that their presence was unnecessary. I was told that leading chorister and solo boy I might be, but my absence would not cause the many letters of complaint that would be received if the Probationers were not present in the "wings". "The ladies adore the dear little boys!" '

In spite of the problems caused by war-time restrictions, various benefactors did their best to entertain the Choristers. Mary Sumner and the Dean gave regular tea-parties, and at Christmas, 'Billy' would invite the Choristers to No.5, to play charades. The boys were also invited to an annual Christmas party at God-Begot House, then a most superior private hotel, where Miss Edith Pamplin would pair them off to dance with girls from St Swithun's School. Miss Pamplin was a Winchester personality of some distinction: she is remembered by generations of Choristers for her regular appearance at their services, clad in black bombazine like a reincarnation of Queen Victoria – an impressive but evidently lovable figure. She died in 1937 and left a considerable bequest to the Cathedral which was used to restore The Pilgrims' School's 'Priory Stabling': she is commemorated by a plaque in the North Transept.

An equally generous benefactress was Mrs. Dorothea Barker, who continued a tradition of hospitality towards the Winchester Cathedral Choristers that had been established by her father, Mr. Charles Boyd. Every year, she organised a 'Primrose Picnic' during Holy Week: boys were taken to Silkstead Lane on Maundy Thursday and would pick primroses to decorate local churches for Easter. They received chocolate Easter eggs as a reward.

Her summer treats were appreciated just as much. The Choristers would walk up St Catherine's Hill, find their tortuous way around the Miz-Maze, then enjoy a strawberry feast in the water meadows below the Hill, so quiet in the blissful days before the by-pass destroyed this part of Hampshire. Then there were parties at Silwood, her large house on the Stockbridge Road, with its organ room built by her father. 'Strawberries and cream were provided in such plenty that one's stomach provided the only curb to the schoolboy's traditional greed!' recalls Jimmy Burchell.

Mrs. Barker died in January 1949 and a number of ex-Choristers attended her funeral, including the celebrated tenor, Eric Greene, who sang a solo.

One other annual event was the autumn expedition to Owslebury: everyone would pick blackberries, and for days afterwards, Colebrook House was filled with the sickly smell of blackberry jam, prepared by the Hone daughters.

Inevitably, the Choristers' most lasting memories are of their duties in the Cathedral. Jimmy Burchell travelled alone by train from Birmingham to Winchester for his voice trial. After a night spent at Colebrook House, 'I was taken to the Cathedral and left sitting on the great oak bench in the South Transept to await my call into the Practice Room. I was overwhelmed by the massive edifice and wondered how my parents had the temerity to think that I could be a chorister in such a wonderful and mighty church! At last I was called in. At the organ was "Billy" Prendergast, looking kindly and benevolent: he gave me confidence right away; but I was not sure about the two clerics sitting in the corner. Later I discovered that one was Dean Furneaux, the other Precentor Wickham. I was asked to sing scales, to read from the Psalms, to sight-read some music. I sang the piece I had brought, which was *I know that my Redeemer liveth*. Then I was sent out to sit on the bench again. I had no hopes and was near to tears as I watched parents being called in. I was the last to be called in again. Billy's first words to me were "Do you need to go home?". I couldn't think what he meant and he laughed and apologised. "You are to be our new solo boy and we want you to start at once because several treble solos are coming up immediately." I was dazed, elated and frightened, all at the same time!'

A complex system of initiation ceremonies welcomed new Choristers. Probationers were put in the old iron-bound chest in the South Transept for a few minutes, then made to crawl between the six marble angels supporting the effigy of Bishop Wilberforce. Then there was 'Stephening': a form of lapidation whereby the luckless probationer was pelted with hymn-books; and, more sophisticated, a ceremony known as 'lifting the crown', the finial which surmounted the Cathedral's coke-stoves. 'New boys were made to stand in front of the stove with one foot on the doors, and press upwards at the same time keeping an eye on the crown. If the boy pressed up hard enough, the ash pan would deposit its contents all over his trousers!'

Of Dr. Prendergast, Philip Sawyer wrote: 'He was a very different type of person from Dr. Arnold and we boys all loved him. He obtained his Doctorate after coming here and there was great excitement when he returned from Oxford and told us that he had obtained very good marks'. 'Billy' was rightly proud of this academic distinction, and would wear his scarlet Doctoral robes in the Close between No.5 and the Cathedral. He was an impressive-looking man, with firm features and a magnificent head of hair, which he used to cover with a skull-cap when in the organ loft or practice room. Normally a shy, rather retiring man, he could nevertheless display an impressive temper when the occasion demanded it. Arthur Barker recalls a disastrous Evensong when the Lay Clerks had inadvertently been issued with a different setting of the *Magnificat and Nunc Dimittis* from that distributed to the boys. 'There was a tremendous crash on the organ, a loud stamping from the organ loft, and a furious white face appeared above the curtain in the organ gallery. Tyack, the bass, made his way out muttering to himself, and a few minutes later returned with the correct copies, after which we all carried on with the same Setting!'

On another occasion, towards the end of 'Billy's' life, the Choir was practising one of his own compositions, a funeral piece for those 'within the veil'. The rehearsal was going badly. Finally, 'Billy' lost his temper, threw the music over the curtains behind him, leant with his forearms on the keys and shouted 'I wish I'd never composed the blooming thing!'

Though perhaps not an outstanding organist by present-day standards, Dr. Prendergast was a good accompanist. He preferred to play the organ himself, and by means of a series of mirrors was able to keep an eye on the Choristers from his loft immediately under the organ pipes. In those days, the organ was blown by a gas engine, installed by Willis in 1887, and during quiet passages one could hear the old single-cylinder engine thumping away. Despite the careful attention of an engineer (who disliked Choristers: 'You boys Houtside!'), the blower occasionally failed – the belt would slip off its pulley with a loud bang. 'That was the signal for emergency services', wrote Arthur Collins. 'Billy would blow a whistle and we each produced a black-covered book which always stayed on the shelves below our desks: it contained a simple, unaccompanied service and an anthem by Goss. Nothing was ever said: we just carried on without the organ.'

Dr. Prendergast seldom conducted the Choir. 'We were so practised that a conductor was not necessary.' The one exception to this rule was when processional hymns were sung at major festivals. 'Dr. Prendergast gave the note on a pitch-pipe and conducted the choir to the stalls. Then he mounted to the organ loft, and the choir was of course dead in tune when the accompaniment came in!'

Many and various are Colebrook Choristers' memories of the Settings and Anthems of the day: staunch Anglican compositions by Stainer, Wesley, Walmisley and their contemporaries for the most part. But as 'Peter' Day recalls, 'One thing stands out above all else: singing the Psalms, morning and evening, throughout the month. All 150 Psalms were thus committed to memory for a life-time'.

Less definable, but equally vivid, are memories of the Cathedral atmosphere: the total darkness of winter evenings, when the only light was in the practice room, and a Chorister might be sent with electric torch to get something from the organ loft for 'Billy'; or winter evensongs by the light of flickering candles and gently-hissing gas mantles; or, in high summer, the evening sunlight streaming down the whole length of the building, picking out the ribbed vaulting in touches of gold.

Chapter Four

FROM COLEBROOK HOUSE TO 'NUMBER NINE'

ONE EVENT that was hardly affected by the Great War was the Southern 'Three Choirs' Festival' involving the combined choirs of Winchester, Chichester and Salisbury, who had first sung together in our Cathedral during the Millennary Celebrations of King Alfred. This festival was a modest enough affair at first, consisting simply of an expanded Evensong in the host cathedral, with one major and two smaller well-known anthems; though Arthur Barker remembers a festival at Winchester when 'we went all modern, and sang *Lord, Thou hast been our Refuge* by Vaughan Williams!'.

The Choristers particularly enjoyed the outing to Salisbury, which was often combined with a trip to Savernake Forest. The large ruffs worn by the Salisbury choristers were considered a great joke by the Winchester boys in the days when they themselves wore Eton collars with their purple cassocks.

In 1917 Dr. Prendergast obtained a new assistant, Miss Hilda Bird. She seldom played the organ when the full Choir was singing, and to most of the Choristers was no more than a disembodied voice. 'I never saw her: I think she lived among the wooden carving of the Quire-screen', recalls Arthur Collins. 'Dickie Bird', as she was inevitably nick-named, used to join 'Billy' in recitals three or four times a year, singing from her favoured position at the west end of the 'Ladies' Gallery' (originally built for Winchester College scholars). 'She had a very loud and coarse soprano voice', recollects one Chorister. However, the boys had reason to be grateful to Miss Bird: the proceeds of the Christmas recital, forerunner of the 'Carol Services' which began in the 1920s, were distributed amongst the Choristers, according to their relative value to the Organist throughout the year. 'Amounts varied from 5/- for a small new boy to £5 10/- for a top solo boy on *Decani*.' Naturally, the Choristers ensured that the Recitals were well attended by distributing hand-bills in the town a few days beforehand, to advertise the forthcoming concert!

Miss Bird was also responsible for an event remembered by Canon Goodman in his article for the *Pilgrims' School Magazine* on the earlier choir schools: a Christmas concert given at Colebrook House in 1923. The programme was ambitious, consisting of piano solos and duets, solo singing, part-songs and carols. The music showed a surprisingly modern choice of composer, English music in the main, including compositions by John Ireland, Ralph Vaughan Williams, Peter Warlock and 'Billy' Prendergast himself. But Miss Bird's days as musical advisor to Colebrook House were numbered: plans to move the Choir School back into the Close were already in hand.

For quite lengthy periods during the First World War, 'Teddy' Hone had been ill, and had relinquished the general running of the school to Percy Spillett, who managed for better or worse. Perhaps the boys respected the unseen presence of their headmaster, sick upon his bed. It was during one of those times that an extra master was recruited, Sidney James, who later married Dorothy Hone. Following his example, Dudley Hone, the youngest of the brothers, married Miss Violet Ings, a matron and junior form teacher, who joined the school after the War when the number of boys had increased somewhat.

Early in 1922 Edward Hone decided to sever his long connection with the Choristers' School. He was a tired and often sick man, and the financial prospects offered by the school were not good. The Hones left Winchester at the end of the year and set up a preparatory school in purpose-built accommodation next to their family home in Mudeford, near Christchurch. The venture was short-lived: three years later, 'Teddy' became ill, went up to London for radiological tests and died there of cancer of the stomach. He was buried in Winchester, at Morne Hill Cemetery, on 14 November 1925.

Meanwhile Percy Spillett found himself, perhaps rather reluctantly, Headmaster of the Choristers' School. He took on a young assistant, Edgar Murray Witham, and a new Matron, Mrs. Farndon. Miss Hilda Bird and the recently-appointed Enid Butler taught the piano.

It soon became clear that Percy Spillett, while admirably suited to being a second master, was no administrator. In his gentle way, he had been the perfect foil to Edward Hone's authoritative personality, but he lacked the firm hand of discipline, so necessary at the time. The Chapter was worried, but Minor-Canon Norman Charles Woods stepped in, volunteering to become 'Warden' of the school, rather along Winchester College lines, thus supervising overall policy at Colebrook House and keeping a careful eye on the boys, while leaving as much of the day-to-day running to Spillett as possible. Minor-Canon Woods visited the school virtually every day: he taught Religious Knowledge, some elementary French or Latin, and he was a regular visitor to the luncheon table.

The arrangement was not altogether satisfactory, least of all for poor 'Spilly', who must have felt that his every move was being scrutinised. There were those on the Chapter who hoped for a 'proper' preparatory school in the Close, to replace the Choristers' School, which seemed to them an amateur affair. In 1925 their plans came to fruition, and Minor-Canon Norman Charles Woods was appointed Headmaster.

Thus 'Spilly' took his seat in the Bournemouth train and joined 'Teddy' in Mudeford for a few months. After Mr. Hone's death, Percy Spillett took over the school, moving with it to other premises in Christchurch. The school was doomed to failure: 'Spilly' ran both it and himself into debt, just as he had done in Winchester, and this time there was no friendly Precentor Wickham and generous Old Choristers' Association to help him out. The school closed, and 'Spilly' was last heard of in Canterbury, earning a meagre living as an elementary school teacher.

So Colebrook House came to an end. The 'odd little school' had produced a number of talented and successful men. In the world of music, these included Eric Greene, whom Sir Reginald Jacques called 'the best Bach tenor in the country' and, in a rather different branch of the art, the versatile musician Felton Rapley, who made his name as a cinema organist of considerable ability, rose to become Manager of the Gaumont-British team of cinema organists and chief Music Arranger at Chappell's, the publishers.

The new Choristers' School was to be at No.9 The Close, a large stone-built edifice, constructed in the 1660s after the Restoration. The Colebrook House classroom block was laboriously dismantled, and re-erected on the south side of Dome Alley, in Dr. Prendergast's stable yard. 'Billy' was furious, and accused the Chapter of not taking him into their confidence: it is said that the Lay Clerks joined in the angry exchange of letters! Finally, Dr. Prendergast appealed to the Cathedral Visitor. The Bishop loyally upheld the Dean and Chapter, and 'Billy' climbed down. When the dust had settled, someone* composed a limerick about the affair:

> Our old *Organorum Pulsator*,
> Of tunes a tremendous *Creator*,
> Though gas fail his bellows
> He'll fail not his fellows
> But will 'gas' like a wild *Agitator*.

Despite these troubles, the school opened on time, and the Choristers moved back into the Close after their 27-year exile. An expensive brochure had been prepared describing the *Cathedral School, Winchester*: Headmaster, Rev. N. C. Woods, M.A., Mus.B. (Selwyn College Cambridge). There were copious illustrations, including a photograph of the schoolroom block taken through a lens of the widest possible angle for maximum effect, and one of the dining room, with tablecloths borrowed for the occasion. The brochure gave details of the fees: £90 a year for boarders and £21 a year for dayboys; but Choristers would have at least half their boarding fees paid by the Chapter.

First on Minor-Canon Woods' 'competent staff' was Edgar Murray Witham, a colourful character and first-class cricket coach, who stayed at No.9 for a regrettably short time before removing to Cambridge and a History degree. He had been in the Flying Corps, and the boys were subjected to regular tests on First War aviators from both sides, and shown his prize possession – the Iron Cross taken from the fuselage of a German aircraft, complete with bullet-holes. John Ford was among his pupils at the Cathedral School:

'He was the proud possessor of a GN sports car in British Racing Green, which made a noise like Concorde and to all appearances travelled at roughly the same speed. After Cambridge, Witham spent the rest of his working life teaching at Wellingborough, and I visited him there on one occasion.

"Whatever became of the GN?" I asked him.

---

* A version of this limerick appears in F. Bussby *Winchester Cathedral* Southampton (Cave) 1979 p. 291, where it is attributed to Canon Madge.

"See that mound over there?" said he, "I buried it with full ceremonial honours. As a matter of fact, it's been down there a good many years now. I'm thinking of digging it up."

'He had a hobby in that he collected the cigarette stubs of the famous. When he had too many for convenience, he distributed them around our cathedrals and important churches. Stubs found their way into the carved ears of reclining dignitaries and, Witham told me, he visited them from time to time. Some of them had been in place for years.'

Murray Witham was involved in a curious episode in 1926. It had been decided to erect a plaque outside Samuel Sebastian Wesley's former house, 9a Kingsgate Street, to commemorate the 50th anniversary of his death. The tablet was quietly affixed in the morning, and that afternoon, the Choir processed down the street to sing an appropriate anthem and watch the Bishop perform the unveiling ceremony. Unfortunately, the Cathedral workmen had been badly briefed and had attached the plaque to the wrong building! Mrs. John Gordon Clark, then Anne Slessor, takes up the tale:

'I had been washing my hair, and used to sit on the roof of No.9 Kingsgate Street, where we then lived, to dry it. I was fascinated that afternoon to see the little ceremony, and even took a photograph of the episode! The birds-eye view shows the Bishop and a small choir.'

That night Murray Witham arrived, tools in hand, and the memorial tablet was attached to the correct house. A few weeks later, he left for Cambridge. He was replaced by a Mr. Charles Townshend: 'An extraordinary soldier of fortune and certainly Irish. He became Headmaster of a school at West Wellow which Lord Melchett seems to have created especially as a preparatory school for his son'.

The second assistant master, John Railton, was a very different character from the colourful Murray Witham. He is described as 'careful, precise, introverted and subtle: the sort of person whose ideas of academic satisfaction were unlikely to be satisfied at number 9'.

The other personality mentioned in the Cathedral School's ambitious brochure was one Sergeant Kempster. 'The boys are drilled twice a week by an ex-Sergeant-Major of the King's Royal Rifle Corps.' The Sergeant, on his retirement from the Army, had taken on the job of groundsman to the entire Wolvesey domain, a post which he retained almost until his death in December 1950. Efficient as a groundsman, his enthusiasm for instructing the young was limited. 'From time to time, perhaps no more than three or four times a term, he used to "take" us for Physical Training. A piece of rope slung over a lower branch of one of the beech trees and a dessicated vaulting horse were about the only equipment and nobody, least of all Kempster, expected anything to come from his – or our – efforts. In any case, the time had long since passed when he himself could pass on the technique of rope-climbing to small and very un-eager boys.'

A relative newcomer to the Choristers' scene was Mr. H. E. Smith, Great War veteran (he held the MC), part-time History teacher at No.9, Scoutmaster of the Bishop's Own Scout Troop, and bass Lay Clerk. He was an accomplished singer and during the early days of broadcasting had sung several solos with the Bourne-mouth Symphony Orchestra. None of these qualifications endeared him to the Choristers, however, and he was resented for 'he had put himself in charge of us, and used to change in our practice room instead of with the men'. This seems a slur on Herbert Smith, who later distinguished himself by his friendly contribution to the musical life and general activities of The Pilgrims' School. Perhaps he was feeling his way into the rôle of a schoolmaster: as one of his early charges recalls, 'He was the Yorkshireman to end all Yorkshiremen when it came to an ability not to disclose his feelings'.

During the six years of its existence, the Cathedral School failed to grow as its creators had hoped and expected. There seem never to have been more than 25 to 30 boys in the school, and the Choristers made up the greater portion of the population. The remainder were almost all dayboys, who disappeared from the premises at 4 o'clock or so.

As far as the Choristers were concerned, life in the Close almost entirely revolved around the Cathedral: only games challenged singing in their list of priorities, and academic activities came a poor third. For teaching purposes, the boys seem to have been divided quite arbitrarily into Seniors and Juniors. Railton took French and Geography, Murray Witham and his successors taught Latin, Maths and English, Mr. Herbert Smith taught some part-time History, and the Headmaster took 'senior Latin' and Scripture.

The late Twenties were uneventful from the Choristers' point of view. The only excitement seems to have been a trip by some senior Choristers to St George's Windsor in 1930, when the 10-year restoration of the Chapel had just been completed. John Hall recalls Sir Walford Davies' instructions to Malcolm Boyle: 'More noise, Malcolm! More! Pull more stops out! Sounds like a blooming harmonium!'

In October 1930 Dean Holden Hutton died. He had been ill for some time, but during his 11-year decanate he had shown unusual interest in the Choristers, more than one of whom still recalls his Christmas Day dinner of 1920, when the entire assembly feasted on stuffed goose. As his obituary in *The Times* noted, 'He loved to have guests at the Deanery, and beyond all, young people'.

Just over two months later, on New Year's Day 1931, Gordon Selwyn was installed Dean of Winchester. He was the son of the Headmaster of Uppingham and had been top scholar of his year at Eton. At Cambridge he had won an impressive number of Classics prizes and had been elected a Fellow of Corpus. He became Warden of Radley, then, forsaking a schoolmaster's career, he took Holy Orders and served for a time as Vicar of Redhill. In due course he was elected Dean of Winchester.

One of his first concerns was the Cathedral School. It was felt in certain quarters that the school had not achieved the expected success, despite the high qualifications of its Head Master. Some wondered whether Minor-Canon Norman Charles Woods was temperamentally suited to the post he had taken up so eagerly. It was decided to take professional advice. Inspectors from the Board of Education were invited to visit the school, and their report proved less than satisfactory. The new Dean acted decisively: the immediate closure of the Cathedral School was announced. It was time to make a fresh start.

The staff went their separate ways. After a year or two, the Reverend N. C. Woods was appointed to the vacant living of Stoke Charity, but he returned to the Cathedral from time to time to play the organ.

Part II

THE PILGRIMS' SCHOOL

Chapter Five

THE FIRST NINE YEARS

THE EVENTS in the Close of 1931 are remembered by many, and though the detail of their accounts may vary, all agree on one fundamental point: Dean Selwyn, scholar, ex-headmaster and priest, had the clearest vision of the sort of school he wished to establish in Winchester (a vision that owed not a little to the choir school of his old college, King's College Cambridge), and from the outset was not prepared to compromise in the fulfilment of that ideal.

So compelling were his convictions that they drew the immediate support of a Chapter not, for the most part, in the prime of youth. With the exception of Canon Madge, who was installed while the new school was being planned, the same members of the Chapter had approved the formation of the previous, unsuccessful Choir School. One Canon, P. H. P. Braithwaite, had joined the Chapter within a few years of the move to Colebrook House, at the turn of the century! Hardly younger was the Cathedral Treasurer and Vice-Dean, Canon Robinson, who proved a most valuable supporter of Dean Selwyn's plans for a new preparatory school in the Close. He was a distinguished ecclesiastical financier, and before the First World War had played a vital rôle in obtaining funds to permit the underpinning of the Cathedral, the famous building operation in which William Walker, the diver, caught the popular imagination.

First, it was necessary to appoint a Headmaster of suitable calibre. One promising candidate was Humphrey Salwey, a young schoolmaster aged 31, son of the Vicar of St John's Church, Meads, in Eastbourne. He was educated at Westminster and won an Exhibition in Classics to Christ Church Oxford; but before going up to University, he obtained a commission in the Grenadier Guards during what proved to be the closing months of the Great War. He taught for some months at his old preparatory school, 'Hill Brow', in Eastbourne, and there discovered his vocation as a schoolmaster. After taking his degree at Oxford, he returned to 'Hill Brow' for three years. His next appointment was at St Wilfrid's School, Bexhill, which was destroyed by fire in 1925 and moved to Hawkhurst under the same name. At this time, Humphrey Salwey had just married Lorna Penruddocke, daughter of the Headmaster of another Eastbourne preparatory school, 'Winchester House', which had started life in Winchester, in a building near the railway station. The young couple boarded rather uncomfortably at the *Eight*

VIII Dean Edward Gordon Selwyn.
A posthumous portrait, presented to the
school in 1962 by his widow

IX Humphrey Salwey. A portrait based on a
photograph taken by his grandson, Roger

X No. 3, The Close in the autumn of 1931. A publicity photograph taken by the Alto
Lay Clerk, Archie Clements

Bells, Hawkhurst, until they could find a suitable house near the school where they were to spend several happy and successful years.

In 1931 Humphrey and Lorna Salwey came to Winchester for the first time and were interviewed by Dean Selwyn at Cheyney Court, for the Deanery was still being redecorated for its new occupant. On a second visit, the Dean wanted to take them to see the house which he hoped would serve as the new school premises: the building which, providentially, had just become vacant following the death of Canon Hepher that January. The visit was inauspicious.

> As so often happens on these occasions, the key was lost: we wandered all around the house, eventually finding an unlatched window – that of the library. We clambered into a dusty, murky house, which seemed to have been empty for several months. We got very little impression of the building!

It was on a subsequent occasion, when Humphrey Salwey and the Dean were standing in Mirabel Close, that the name of the new school was decided.

> The Dean wanted to get away from the words 'Cathedral', 'Choir' and so on, and find something original. I became rather tired of making somewhat feeble suggestions, so rather to change the subject, I asked him what the old building was to the left of the front door, into which the house seemed to be built, and he said 'Oh, that's the Pilgrims' Hall'. We then looked at each other; because obviously you couldn't have a better name than that for small boys starting out on their voyage through life. I told him there was another 'Pilgrims School' at Seaford in Sussex, and he replied, 'Well then, let this be THE Pilgrims' School!' Thus the name was born.

Humphrey Salwey was short-listed and attended the final selection interview in the Chapter Room. 'About the only thing I can remember about the meeting', he said later, 'was that Canon Braithwaite, a rather lugubrious man with a long white beard, said that "he hoped boys would possibly obtain scholarships".'

Shortly afterwards, Mr. Salwey was appointed Headmaster of The Pilgrims' School. At the Dean's request, Humphrey and Lorna Salwey visited the choir school of King's College to learn more about the running of such foundations. The Pilgrims' School was to open in September 1931, under an unwritten agreement that the school would run experimentally for three years on trial.

No.3 The Close had little to commend it for its new purpose, least of all its size. Present generations of Pilgrims would undoubtedly be surprised at the smallness of the building as it was in 1931, and as it appeared in the frontispiece to every number of the *School Magazine* during Humphrey Salwey's headmastership, reminding readers of the school's humble beginnings, before the skilfully-matched New Wing containing the dining room and main school classrooms was added. Only the 'aboriginals' – the boys who moved to No.3 from the 'Cathedral School' – will remember the southern end of the house as it appears in an early photograph (p.54), one of a series taken by 'Archie' Clements in September 1931 for publicity purposes. The Victorian verandah and conservatory were demolished a year later to make way for the New Wing, and the blind openings still visible inside the building are the only vestiges of the former first-floor windows.

Some 55 yards to the south of the conservatory was the stable block of No.3, now the changing room. Many an early Pilgrim recalls the tortuous path through the shrubbery which separated the two buildings: a hazardous journey, it seems, particularly at night, when the path was lit only by a feeble outside light at either end.

The stable block consisted of two stalls and a loose-box, with a large hay-loft above, and an adjacent harness-room. To the right of the stables, built against the wall of the Close, was an old coach-house, which was turned into a double garage. A wall running parallel and close to the 16th-century Priory Stables separated that building from the stable yard of No.3; a return wall, at right-angles to the Priory Stables, enclosed the cathedral builders' yard; and the maintenance staff used much of the ground floor of the derelict stabling itself. Thus the Yard of No.3, now so active as forum, roller-skating rink and football or cricket pitch, was but a third of its present size; and so it would remain for a further 30 years.

Such was the domain inherited by the newly-founded Pilgrims' School in the summer of 1931. Much had to be done before the buildings were ready for occupation, not least the cleaning of the house – a formidable task, undertaken by Mrs. Ada Pain, the first appointment to the domestic staff. She was still working when the Salweys retired, 32 years later, as was Eddie Grace, whose association with The Pilgrims' School began shortly after World War Two and continued until 1978. Such devoted service was typical of the loyal support that Lorna Salwey, in sole command of the domestic and catering arrangements, received from so many members of her staff.

Time was short, money scarce, and the venture still on trial: very little building work took place during the months before the school opened. The stable block was converted into a changing room, the hay-loft was converted into accommodation for two resident masters by the addition of dormer windows. There were just two bedrooms and a bathroom, reached by a wooden open-tread staircase outside the building, little more than a ladder, and treacherously slippery in wet weather. The harness-room became a small Common Room with an oppressively low ceiling.

No other alterations were needed before the school opened. The dining room was established in the present 'Dorm II', the largest room in the house, with pleasant views across the Close from the big north-facing windows, and down the garden from the bay-window on the eastern side, above the conservatory. As the dining room was on the first floor, food had to be brought up from the kitchens below in a service lift, whose redundant hatch remains in the basement corridors. One of 'Archie' Clements' photographs shows the elegant room set for lunch, with flowers on the tables. These tables, together with benches, desks, chairs and other items of school furniture, had been brought over from No.9 during the summer holidays.

Another photograph shows the Cathedral School beds in their new home. 'Dorm I' must have been a delightfully airy room in those days, with its south-facing bay-window looking towards the College. Unfortunately, there was not room for all 22 'aboriginals' to sleep in the school. The one dormitory accommodated about ten boys; others were put up in the 'private side', but some had to sleep out at the Deanery or in Cheyney Court. In the enthusiasm to get the school started, the 'Advisory Council' had estimated that the house could comfortably contain 44 boys or so, but they had completely overlooked the fact that the Headmaster and his family would also require rooms on the school premises!

Classroom space was equally limited. There were just two available rooms in No.3: the Library and the adjoining morning room.* After the New Wing was completed, it was possible to restore the Library to its original function, although it had to double as a junior classroom for some years, and then as a handicrafts room. This elegantly panelled room has now been adapted for use as a television room, both for recreational and educational purposes.

Fortunately, the newly-founded school was able to retain the use of the classrooms in Dome Alley, which remained a valuable annexe to the school's facilities until the late Fifties, by which time, as one 'reputable young mathematician' calculated, the Headmaster had walked more than 1687.5 miles to and from his classroom! The apparently meaningless cry of 'In or Over!', by which prefects signal the end of morning break and the resumption of afternoon school, is a relic of the days when boys had either to 'go in' to the main school building or 'go over' to Dome Alley.

The school's sporting facilities consisted of the playing field in front of the Bishop's Palace, known as Wolvesey field, which in earlier years had been used by the Choristers of Colebrook House and No.9 The Close. Only half the present playing area was available, for a fence separated 'Wolvesey' from Bailey's market garden at the north end of the meadow, while both the present junior pitch and the Bishop's orchard next to the castle ruins were occupied by the courts leased to the Winchester Tennis Club.

The Pilgrims' School opened on Friday 18 September 1931 with just 22 boys. Fifteen were Choristers, five were Probationers, one was a Chorister whose voice had broken during the holidays, and the youngest was the son of Canon Hodgson, who had replaced Canon Hepher on the Chapter. The boys were divided into two 'Sets' to provide a competitive element in sport: these were known as the 'Monks' after the inhabitants of the Close before the Reformation, and the 'Wrens' after the supposed architect of the school buildings. There were just two assistant masters, and the boys were divided into three forms.

Ten days after the school opened, the Bishop of Winchester conducted a special service in the upstairs dining room, dedicating the school 'To the Glory of God and the Service of His Church'. He was fated to see little of the development of the school which had received his blessing: staff and boys were saddened by the news of his death the following February. After the dedication ceremony, Dean Selwyn spoke to the parents, expressing the hope that the school might be 'a little Winchester within the Close: a school with a great future'. Also present were the other members of the Chapter, who made up the Governing Body of the school: the Vice-Dean, Canon Robinson; Canon Braithwaite; Cecil Boutflower, the Bishop of Southampton − a loyal supporter of the school in its infancy, who frequently came to lecture on a variety of subjects; and Canon Hodgson, The Pilgrims' School's first dayboy parent.

* The present Bursary.

47

Equally important guests were the members of the 'Advisory Council', which the Dean and Chapter had established to assist them in forming the school's educational policy. The Council consisted of the Dean, the two senior Canons, the Headmaster of Winchester College, the retired Headmaster of a well-known preparatory school, Mr. Bernard Rendall, who later apologised for being responsible for the miscalculation of the capacity of the school buildings, and a Secretary to the Council, Mr. J. P. Graham, who had been Second Master at Uppingham during the headmastership of Dean Selwyn's father.

Dr. Prendergast, Organist and Master of the Choristers, had also been closely consulted during the early stages of the new venture. It will be recalled that six years earlier, Dr. Prendergast had been excluded from the discussions concerning the formation of the 'Choir School';the Cathedral Visitor, Bishop Frank Theodore Woods, had regretted this omission. 'Billy' Prendergast proved a loyal supporter of The Pilgrims' School, and agreed to certain compromises in order to facilitate a timetable which would take into account an increasing number of Commoner boarders. The boys' required attendances at Mattins were reduced to two per week, and the morning practice was moved back half an hour, to 8.30, so that lessons could start at 9.00.

Perhaps the most valuable inclusion in the Advisory Council was that of Dr. Alwyn Williams, Headmaster of Winchester College and later Bishop of Winchester. It was he who, at the first meeting of the Council, granted The Pilgrims' School the use of the College Gymnasium from January 1932. A few moments later, he expressed a hope that the new school might accept as dayboys the sons of any College dons who might wish to send them there. Humphrey Salwey, who earlier at the meeting had said 'Of course there will be no dayboys', hurriedly ate his words, and a valuable link was forged.

In spite of Dr. Williams' encouragement, it was hard to sell the school to prospective parents at first. There was so little for them to see: a dining room, a dormitory and two small classrooms. Dome Alley was too far to take parents, and the Wolvesey playing field even further, for in those days there was no short cut via the 'garden gate'.

Humphrey Salwey recalls another amusing aspect of his interviews with prospective parents.

> At that time, I looked a bit younger than I actually was, and I remember at least two occasions when the conversation was slow, and I was trying to answer the questions that I thought a prospective parent ought to be asking, when one or other of them would look at me and say, 'Well, of course we *really* want to see the Headmaster!'

The fees at least were attractive, particularly for Choristers. In 1931 the Commoner fees were only £105 *per annum*, Chorister fees only £30! The Dean was anxious that the school should not be an expensive one, but the Headmaster had to enlighten one or two parents who asked, 'There must be a snag in this: do you feed the boys properly?'.

The boys undoubtedly *were* fed properly, under the careful supervision of Lorna Salwey, in marked contrast with previous *régimes*. Two of the so-called 'aboriginals', who had transferred from No.9, were able to compare old and new. After

48

XI The Choristers, October 1931, with Dr. Prendergast and Miss Hilda Bird. Front row (*left to right*): Curwen, Dark, Ollerenshaw, Morse; second row: Crosley, Wake, Rooke, Miss Bird, Dr Prendergast, Buckett, Goodale, Graham; third row: Hicks, Farley, Longuet-Higgins, Varley, Kendall, Standbridge, Fairbairn, Hunter, Prentice I, Kemp Robinson, Leonard

XII The Pilgrims' School, June 1934. Front Row (*left to right*): Cate, Cussans, Ley, Earle II, Cronk, Michael Salwey, Brown, Foster, McDonald, Payne, Burrett, Dark; second row: Hunter, Goodale, Mr. Phipps, Mr. Scott, Mrs. Salwey, Mr. Salwey, Mr. Payton, Sister Cheal, Graham, Buckett; third row: Earle I, Balfour, Longuet-Higgins, Smith, Farley, Crosley, Varley, Fairbairn, Tayler, Chambers, Ollerenshaw, Kemp Robinson; back row: Hodgson, Spencer, Arnold, Hicks, Prentice I, Leonard, Aston, Caesar, Morse, Prentice II, Eve, Verry

a term or two, Desmond Farley and John Hunter were chatting together and recalled that they had not yet raided the kitchen, a nocturnal activity of the old Choir School that was almost essential to survival.

'Perhaps we're gooder', said Farley.

'Not at all', replied Hunter, 'We're simply better fed'. Desmond Farley, later to distinguish himself in the field of medicine, considers this his first lesson in human physiology.

During those early terms, football was the only winter sport, but it was hard to break into the crammed fixture lists of established preparatory schools in the area. The first match, against the Quirister School, ended in defeat; but this minor set-back was reversed in the return match, with a magnificent 16-2 victory. Westbury House was defeated twice, with final scores of 6-4, then 10-nil! These were results that augured well for the development of Pilgrims' sport.

A pattern of winter activities began to develop. There were frequent lectures, including two talks on the Solar System by Mr. Stawell Brown, who, first as friend and later as parent, took a benevolent interest in the school and was responsible for building up a fascinating collection of lantern slides (difficult to project these days, now that 2½ in. format has gone out of fashion) showing the daily life of the school during the first 20 years of its existence. Some lecturers returned again and again: like Miss Newbury, formerly a missionary in China, who visited the school no fewer than 28 times to talk on a variety of historical and geographical subjects. A notable coup was the successful invitation to Mr. Edward Shackleton to talk on the 'Oxford University Expedition to Ellesmere Land'.

There were more light-hearted activities: the first Pilgrims' 'At Home', when boys, parents and friends were entertained with conjuring tricks; the Guy Fawkes celebrations on Wolvesey; while at Christmas the Choristers were invited to a 'Hogmanay Party' at the Deanery, forerunner of the 'Turkey Feast', instituted the following year. During the Easter term, while the more intellectually inclined enjoyed the mental challenge provided by the chess or draughts competition, others could try to win a prize for that now extinct game, 'Tenikoits'.

In 1932 Pilgrims' boys first enjoyed Dr. Alwyn Williams' offer, and began regular gym classes under the College P.T. Instructor, Mr. Gear: a considerable change from Sergeant Kempster's half-hearted activities. 'P.T. was great fun, except for those nasty wooden horses, against which one could bark one's shins rather severely', recalls Anthony Caesar, who, as Head Boy in 1938, presented a silver biscuit box to Mr. Gear on behalf of the school. Mr. Gear's 'retirement' proved to be short-lived: at the outbreak of War, his successor rejoined the Army, and he took up his duties at the College gym once more, until 1945.

Less pleasant are Anthony Caesar's memories of early morning cold showers in the changing room during the summer term. 'There we were, in a long line, utterly silent and entirely naked, waiting our turn to enter the dreaded shower bath hissing with freezing water. Meanwhile the Headmaster was most comfortably attired in pyjamas and warm dressing-gown calling out NEXT – until (and beyond) that famous day when eldest son Michael, then seven or eight years old perhaps, cried out in front of the whole solemn assembly: "Daddy, why don't *you* have a shower!" '

The standard of cricket was low at first: the traditions established by 'Spilly' and Murray Witham had long been forgotten. Patiently, Humphrey Salwey began laying the foundations again. One of the ways he encouraged accurate bowling was by awarding chocolate for 'good-length balls', which had hit a metal plate in the ground, towards the end of a practice wicket on the lawn behind the house. During the War, chocolate was of course unavailable, and money took its place. A penny was the reward for hitting the plate, or the hat-trick, and the total amount won was recorded yearly in the *Magazine*. The system was commended by Harry Altham in an article written at Humphrey Salwey's retirement. He saw in it a paradigm of the Headmaster's educational philosophy:

'How many young bowlers have been helped to find length and direction by the "tin-plate" challenge and reward? Yet here, too, there was no compromise: a "near miss" was just no good'.

Athletics did not occupy its present place as a rival and alternative to cricket until 1968. The school 'Sports' took place at the beginning of the Half-Term weekend, and during the previous week Set Masters would instruct their teams as best as the limited time would allow. In 1932, the Competition was between the Monks and the Wrens alone, there being but two Sets, and the Wrens were the first winners of the challenge cup presented by Mrs. Salwey. In spite of a plethora of cups of all shapes and sizes, presented by willing parents, the original philosophy of 'The Sports' has survived, the ideal which for years appeared in the printed programme: 'The Athletic Cup will be awarded, not to an individual performer, but to the Set which gains the highest aggregate of points in the Sports. Thus although the winners of individual events will receive mementos in the usual way, the main effort will be for the Set, and the personal success will be of incidental importance'.

During its first summer term, the school gained an influential ally at the Judges' Lodgings: Mr. Justice Charles, who frequently took the Western Circuit before the War and showed a benevolent interest in the school. His association with The Pilgrims' School started when he and Mr. Justice Amory attended Mattins in the Cathedral on the Sunday following their arrival. So delighted were they with the singing that they asked for a half-holiday, a popular request that was to be repeated many times. Mr. Justice Charles was a regular visitor to the Wolvesey cricket ground, and he also took a keen interest in swimming. It was he who presented the challenge cup for diving, in 1936.

Other significant, but otherwise unrelated, events towards the end of the year included the enthronement of Cyril Garbett as the new Bishop of Winchester, 'severe and shy, with sonorous voice and princely manner, destined for high office as Archbishop', as Anthony Caesar describes him; and a visit to the Winchester Amateur Operatic Society's production of *The Yeomen of the Guard*, conducted by no less a personage than Mr. Malcolm Sargent.

Thus the first year came to an end, marred for the Salweys by the death of their second son, David.

The school had grown somewhat during the previous 10 months, to a total of 28 boys, but academic standards were modest. The top mark in the trial Common Entrance Examination was 35 per cent. Whether these results were communicated to the Dean and Chapter is not known. Nevertheless, after only a third of the trial period had passed, the Cathedral authorities showed sufficient confidence in the school to approve the plans for a New Wing to be added to the premises, which would contain a dining room, new classrooms, dormitories and other facilities.

'At last we had something to show to prospective parents, and something to look forward to', Humphrey Salwey wrote later.

In this way, the new school year opened on an optimistic note. An increasingly large circle of friends, as well as parents, were becoming interested in the life of the school, and at the first Entertainment, early in December 1932, there was an audience of more than 250 people. The musical programme consisted of piano pieces, solo singing and part-songs, including two compositions by Dr. Prendergast; but more memorable still were the 'Scenes from *Macbeth*'. Jack Graham's performance as Lady Macbeth made a considerable impression on the audience and, in retrospect, the surviving photographs of this production are made more poignant by the knowledge that this talented boy was shot down and killed in the War, less than 10 years later.

Christmas came round again, and the Salweys ensured that the Choristers, who remained in Winchester until the first Sunday of the New Year, enjoyed themselves to the full: the house was decorated, stockings were hung up in the dormitories – and generously filled – and the traditional Christmas fare was provided in abundance. In 1932 the celebrations were postponed until Boxing Day, for on Christmas Day itself the Choir gave its first broadcast: a special service which went out over the national transmitter at 8 o'clock in the evening. A few days later, Dean Selwyn invited the Choristers to a party at the Deanery, and the 'Waterloo Cup' was instituted. This is a competition between *Decani* and *Cantoris* who, as in the Cathedral, sit in two rows facing each other, but with forearms crossed and palms uppermost. At the Dean's command of 'go!', a coin is placed in the nearer palm of each end boy; he must transfer it to his other palm, thence to the nearest hand of his neighbour, and thus down the row and back, hand over hand. A practised team can achieve this in a surprisingly short time. The best of three rounds wins the 'cup': the remains of a German tin-plate toy consisting of two birds who 'bill' when their bellows are pressed but have long since lost the ability to 'coo'. The absurdity of title and trophy have no doubt contributed to the perpetuation of this annual ritual for over 60 years.

This Christmas was to be Dr. Prendergast's last: he died on 20 February 1933. Organist for over 30 years, he had seen many changes in the arrangements made for the education of his Choristers, but particularly warm was his support for The Pilgrims' School. The Dean of Winchester wrote: 'He allowed no interest of his own to come before the welfare of his choir. When in 1931 The Pilgrims' School was established on a full preparatory basis, with the Choristers as choral scholars, he threw himself unstintingly into the new order, and contributed greatly by his enthusiasm to its success'.

So it was that Anthony Caesar never sang under the Organist who had accepted him at the voice trials 'at the third attempt; and the boy is still left with the uncomfortable feeling that he must somehow have hastened him to his grave'.

Dr. Prendergast's continuing legacy to the Cathedral is his collection of seasonal Antiphons, one of which is sung daily in the South Transept at the start of Evensong.

Mr. Theodore Walrond, the Organist of St Cross, stood in during the interregnum. Miss Hilda Bird, who had been 'Billy's' faithful assistant since 1917, remained for a few months, but resigned before the new Organist was appointed.

Meanwhile work was going ahead on the New Wing, designed by a local architect, Mr. Harold Sawyer. The builders cleared the trees and bushes between the conservatory and the changing room, and began to dig foundations. The building works involved excavating to a considerable depth, particularly at the southern end of the building, where an underground boiler room was planned below the Senior Classroom. During the course of the excavations, various archaeological discoveries were unearthed, which illustrated most tellingly that the site had been occupied since prehistoric times. There were animal remains, notably bone fragments from the Celtic Ox, *Bos longifrons*, whose evocative Latin name caught the imagination of the boys; fragments of Belgic pottery; the foundations of a Roman building and several Roman coins dating from the third century A.D.; pottery fragments from the Middle Ages; and medieval 'jettons', a relic of the commercial activity of St Swithun's Priory. These finds were fully described in the *School Magazine* by Sidney Ward-Evans, Winchester's 'Honorary Archaeologist'; he later arranged a permanent exhibition of the discoveries, which were mounted in the dining room in display cases provided through the generosity of the parents.

It was a wet spring, and archaeological investigations were quickly curtailed as the pit dug for the heating chamber filled with water. A pump ran continuously but could only just cope with the flow of water into the excavations – the water table lies close under the surface of this low-lying part of Winchester, as the annual flooding of the Cathedral Crypt shows. A similar problem was to beset the architect of the Selwyn Building, 40 years later.

On Thursday 30 March 1933, the Headmaster of Merchant Taylors' School, Mr. Spencer Leeson, laid the foundation stone of the new building. The weather continued wet and the proceedings had to be transferred to the old dining room upstairs, the stone itself being laid during a lull in the storm. This was the start of Mr. Spencer Leeson's valuable association with The Pilgrims' School, for two years later he took up his appointment as Headmaster of Winchester College, in succession to Dr. Alwyn Williams.

During the summer of 1933, another small but useful building operation took place. Despite some opposition from Canon Braithwaite, who talked gloomily of 'this breach in our battlements', the Dean and Chapter allowed an opening to be pierced in the Close Wall at the end of the garden, thus considerably shortening the journey between the school buildings and the playing fields. In this way an old privilege, obtained by a previous inhabitant of the house in 1664, was renewed.

The New Wing was completed in commendably short time and, although the start of the school year had to be delayed, the extension was ready for occupation on the first day of term, 22 September. 'The first few hours after arrival were a time of exploration and discovery', wrote the Headmaster in the *Magazine*. There was the new dining room to get used to, with space for up to 70 boys if necessary, while the old dining room was turned into a second dormitory. Separated from the dining room by a folding partition was the 'junior classroom': the two rooms could be turned into one large hall when needed. The senior classroom next door completed this valuable addition to the school's teaching facilities. Upstairs were two further dormitories, a washroom and four bathrooms, a sick-bay and accommodation for the Matron. The corridors on either floor were joined to the existing

XIII South end of the School buildings in 1931, before the addition of the New Wing

XIV An amazing score, amassed during a Staff Match. Adults include (*wearing ties, left to right*) Vincent Phipps, Vincent Payton and Tom Scott

passages although a short flight of stairs had to be built to accommodate the difference in floor level. There was a new 'front door' for the boys and leading from the boys' hall, a boot-room (now known as 'Toyes') for shoes, coats and caps.

On Sunday 1 October Dr. Garbett, now in his second year as Bishop of Winchester, performed a short service of dedication in the dining room. The following Saturday the Wing was officially opened by Major-General Sir John Capper, in the presence of the Dean and Chapter, the Advisory Council and about 300 parents and well-wishers. This was the first time that the 'School Hall' had been used, and it proved adequate for the occasion.

The New Wing possessed a long attic which served as a box-room, and this proved an ideal site for the shooting range. Air-rifle shooting had started the previous Easter term, in the loft of the Priory Stable Block, which was repaired somewhat for that purpose by the Friends of the Cathedral; at that time, the Stables were otherwise no part of the school premises. From these modest beginnings developed one of the school's most successful sports: between 1941 and 1959, The Pilgrims' was to win the inter-school trophy known as the 'St David's Shield' over 20 times.

Boxing was another sport that could be practised in the new extension, and the attachment points for the ropes of the school boxing ring may still be seen in the dining room and junior common room. 'Mr. Gear achieved the near impossible and got us actually to enjoy boxing on winter Saturday evenings', recalls Anthony Caesar. Indeed, the enthusiasm was considerable, and during the first term, three quarters of the school joined the classes. There was an informal display at the end of 1933, but the main Boxing Competitions took place at the end of the Easter term. A few years later, the annual Boxing Mix-up was instituted, giving nearly every boy in the school the opportunity of boxing at least one round. Gradually, in the late 1960s, the sport fell out of fashion, and in 1970 it gave way to Judo – the 'Gentle Art' – under Jim Bates of Winchester College.

Meanwhile, the Choristers had a new Organist and Master, Dr. Harold Rhodes, formerly Organist of Coventry Cathedral. Anthony Caesar remembers a man 'who could indeed command in the musical sense, but was most gentle by nature. It must have been the hardest thing for him ever to reprimand: even now, I can see the pain on his face when two of us behaved boorishly during a practice'.

At the end of his first term at Winchester, Dr. Rhodes conducted the Choir in a new radio venture, the 'Bells of Bethlehem' broadcast on Christmas Eve. 'For a quarter of an hour, Bethlehem, London, New York and Winchester were linked up, and Europe and America listened to one of the most moving broadcasts that have been given.' The programme included a perfectly synchronised rendering of *O come, all ye faithful*, in which the New York choir sang the first and last verses while Winchester sang the second and third. Later, a letter of appreciation was received from a Mr. and Mrs. B. Thorn, who lived in Alberta. 'Sitting very comfortably by the radio, with the thermometer registering 35° below zero outside, it took us back to our childhood days in good old Winchester where both my wife and I were born.'

Earlier that term, the school had gained another influential benefactor: the Lord Lieutenant of Hampshire, Lord Mottistone, formerly General Seely. He had visited the school to present a prize awarded for the best essay on his book *Fear and be slain*. At the ceremony, he described his recent interviews with Herr Hitler and Signor Mussolini, and offered his own annual 'Lord Lieutenant's Prize' to replace Dean Selwyn's award. By way of returning the compliment, the Dean's own book, *The Story of Winchester Cathedral*, was the text set in 1934. Lord Mottistone was to become an esteemed friend of the school. During the War he spent many months each year living at the Judges' Lodgings, and in 1942 he contributed a nostalgic article, 'Memories' to the *Magazine*:

> I have spent many years in different wars; and my greatest consolation was the memory of beautiful sights and sounds in the happy days at home. One thing particularly I beg of you to appreciate now so that you may cherish it as a memory: the sound of wind in the trees. There is a different sound for each tree and for the different times of the year; and just as the sea near where I live is sometimes a murmur, sometimes a mighty roar, so it is with trees in a great storm, when the elms and limes outside The Pilgrims' School are swaying about in the wind.

By the summer of 1934, the number of boys in the school had risen to 39 and a new class was formed. That term two new masters joined the staff: Vincent Phipps, whose dynamic career as a schoolmaster came to an untimely end when he joined the Coldstream Guards in 1940; and Vincent Payton, whose mathematical enthusiasm was matched only by a passion for cricket, which he imparted to the boys in equal measure. Nor were Mr. Payton's sporting abilities confined to summer sports, for six months later he introduced the boys to hockey, which has attracted an enthusiastic following ever since. While Vincent Payton took over the Wrens Set, Vincent Phipps was the first Master of a new Set, the 'Romans', named after the early inhabitants of The Pilgrims' School site, whose remains had been discovered during the excavations, a year or two previously.

That summer the Wrens won the School Sports for the third year running, and in the face of impressive coaching, for both Mr. Scott of the Monks and Mr. Phipps of the Romans had been Presidents of the Athletic Clubs of their respective Oxbridge colleges.

As the school entered its fourth year, it was clear that Humphrey Salwey's insistence that 'nothing but the best would do' was beginning to produce academic success. In 1933 the first scholarship was won, to Brighton College. This was followed by three awards a year later, including a scholarship to Westminster. These achievements must be attributed to the Headmaster's rejection of the second-rate, and his close personal supervision of every aspect of the boys' life.

> I particularly wanted to teach once a week in all the classes to see how they were getting on, and not always depend on what I was told. After the War, the school got too big for that sort of thing. But I enjoyed it, and it seemed to me the right thing to do.

Thus, as Anthony Caesar recalls, 'within the school, the Headmaster loomed very large indeed, and he and his wife, from our limited view-point, managed to complement each other in a very wonderful way'.

56

XIV Dean and Chapter cricket match vs. The Pilgrims' School, 17 July 1934

XVI Sports Day at Wolvesey, 22 June 1935

XVII Humphrey Salwey and Leavers, summer 1938

The *régime* was strict, but as Mrs. Gordon Selwyn observed later: 'One was struck by the boys' confident approach to their Headmaster. In their opinion he was strict but just: justice and fairness was the yardstick by which they assessed him, and if they transgressed, as on occasions they did, they knew exactly where they were'.

The staff shared their Headmaster's philosophy. The firm discipline came as a shock to one new boy, who wrote home after a very short time at the school:

> I don't like the rules here nearly as much as the rules at Field Place. There are two assistant masters, one I like, but the other which is the French master I don't like at all, he is too strict. He makes me do extra French work in all my spare time, straight after lunch he makes me work, before my meals digest.

As Neville Ollerenshaw explained later: 'All this refers to Tom Scott: he earned my unqualified admiration before I left the school'.

In this disciplined framework, academic potential could be fulfilled. The scholarship boys were 'stretched' by the extra coaching of Mr. Blakeney, the former Headmaster of Ely Grammar School, who had retired to Winchester. However, Humphrey Salwey was not interested only in brilliant academic achievements, satisfying though the lengthening list of public school awards might be. 'Greater still was the pleasure of seeing those who were less gifted academically passing happily into their next schools and later prospering greatly.'

A great boost to the morale of Headmaster and staff alike was the visit, in February 1935, of two Inspectors from the Board of Education. Naturally, there was some apprehension before these gentlemen arrived, and Humphrey Salwey, who had not been 'inspected' during his two previous teaching posts, knew no more what to expect than his staff did. When Mr. Firkins and Mr. Morley arrived, they confessed that this was their first experience of this kind of school. They were intrigued by the complexity of the timetable and spent a considerable amount of time talking with the Headmaster. Indeed, they had to be encouraged to sit in on lessons, but they proved most friendly and co-operative, and wrote a very favourable report, in which many of the plans for the future development of the school which Humphrey Salwey had outlined to the Inspectors were included under the heading of 'suggestions'. Thus the school was 'recognised as efficient'. Mr. Firkins became a friend of the school, attending the Handicrafts Exhibition the following year, and distributing the prizes on Sports Day in 1937.

In their report, the Inspectors made special mention of the Library founded by Tom Scott: this had grown rapidly through the generosity of parents. It contained books to suit all tastes, and had been created on the principle that boys should learn to enjoy reading, be it nothing more high-brow than *The Dormitory Flag*, *Off to the Wicket* or *The Gayton Scholarship*, titles typical of a minor literary genre that has died since the last War.

The event which really established the academic reputation of The Pilgrims' School came after the Inspection, however. In May 1935, H. C. Longuet-Higgins was placed 'Head of the Roll' in the Winchester College Election. He was the first Pilgrim to attempt the examination, and so none of the staff had any idea of the required standard. The Headmaster was delighted to learn that he had reached the second round and was required for interview.

Then we had to wait until noon on Saturday, when the 'Roll came down', which meant that it was posted in the College Porter's Lodge. I remember going along that morning; and being a humble-minded sort of person, I started at the bottom of the list and went slowly up, feeling more and more depressed as he didn't seem to be there. I couldn't believe my eyes when I discovered he'd got the top place!

After this success Longuet-Higgins, a Chorister and 'solo boy', amused himself by composing an *Evening Service in F* which was sung in the Cathedral on August Bank Holiday.

Over 20 years later, the first Winchester scholar, by then Professor of Theoretical Chemistry at Cambridge, returned to Winchester to speak at the school's Silver Jubilee celebrations. By that date, the number of boys listed on the Honours Board first presented by his parents totalled 103, including 16 scholarships to Winchester College and a second 'Head of the Roll'.

It was during the summer term of 1935 that Chorister Guy Kemp Robinson found himself locked in the Cathedral, after gathering up the books after Evensong. 'Inspiration came to him', recalls Anthony Cussans, 'and he went into the organ loft and played loudly. The Dean heard the sound but assumed that one of Dr. Rhodes' pupils was practising. Kemp Robinson, who by this time was getting rather alarmed, switched from "Sacred" music to *The Isle of Capri*. The Dean, horrified, hurried in through the side door in the Slype and found a white-faced little boy at the organ. Dean Selwyn always recognised initiative and any form of originality, and promptly congratulated Guy and restored him to the warmth and safety of the school'. Needless to say, his fellow-Choristers were convinced that he had got himself 'locked in' on purpose, so as to play the organ!

Late in July 1935 the school held its first 'Swimming Sports'. Swimming still took place in the Bull Drove Baths, as it had done since the beginning of the century, and the weather determined the start of the swimming season, which seldom opened much before the end of June. Anthony Caesar recalls the weekly trek to the baths, on Friday mornings: 'The charm of the surroundings in the Meads was largely off-set by the muddy and uncertain nature of the bottom, which made the always cool Itchen water rather a fearful thing, like Psalm 69: "I stick fast in the deep mire where no ground is"'!

Nevertheless, boys learned to swim quite rapidly (a question of necessity in such conditions), and a system of 'stars' for swimming proficiency had been introduced the previous summer. As luck would have it, two of the school's strongest swimmers were in the newly-formed Romans Set, who won the Sports for the first time.

Two days after those Swimming Sports, on 26 July, the Choristers, Lay Clerks, Organist, Sacrist, Dean and Headmaster left Southampton by the night boat, bound for the Channel Islands on a trip to the remotest corner of the Winchester Diocese in aid of the Cathedral Appeal fund. It was the boys' second voyage down Southampton Water that month: less than a fortnight earlier, they had cruised among the Fleet at the Spithead Review in the boat *Joybell III*, and some, alas, had been sea-sick.

That fact probably accounts for the insistent note in Neville Ollerenshaw's dramatic description of the choir trip in his schoolboy publication, the *Jersey Number* of *The Good Companions*.

'At 5.00 a.m. we woke up and just lay and felt, some of us, a touch of *mal de mer*: Prentice i and Eve actually were, and rumours went round that I was, *but the rumours were wrong*.'

Later, at the entrance to St Helier harbour, 'We threw bits of biscuits to the sea-gulls, and they caught them in mid-air, thereby reminding us of Mr. Payton, our Maths and Cricket master, who is a posh catch: so we named one of the gulls after him'.

The boys were taken to the private homes where they were to stay, and then driven to the Havre des Pas swimming pool to bathe, before changing into Marlborough suits for their first concert at the house of Lady Trent and her daughter, the Hon. Molly Boot. This apparently somewhat disappointing secular engagement in the garden of the heiress to Boot's Cash Chemists was followed by a late Evensong in St Matthew's, the church which Lady Trent had built in memory of her husband.

'This was a hazardous affair', as Anthony Cussans remembers, 'since Lalique had been employed to decorate a good deal of the interior with his fabulous glass, which, we were told, would shatter if we sang certain notes. So Dr. Rhodes had to select "suitable" music so as not to leave the church in ruins.'

Next day, after Communion at St Mark's Church, the Choir visited Corbière lighthouse, where the two rather ancient lighthouse keepers asked if 'this choir from England' could sing the National Anthem for them? We all stood on the spiral staircase desperately trying to remember the words of verses two and three. But the old chaps seemed satisfied!'

The Choir set off for Guernsey the next morning. There, the boys were accommodated at St Elizabeth College, where they quickly discovered a piano and a piano accordion, on each of which they played *Does Santa Claus sleep with his whiskers on?* several times! Everyone visited the town and, in the afternoon, made an unscheduled visit to Herm, described by Humphrey Salwey:

'While we were in Guernsey, their Dean was going to that wonderful island of Herm to conduct a baptism in a tiny chapel on the island, and it was thought that there had probably never been a baptism there before. Some kind friend provided a large enough boat, and we all went over; the Choir sang something suitable for this little service, and then we all spent some time on a fascinating coral beach nearby.'

This visit nearly ended in tragedy, as the editor of *The Good Companions* relates:

We had a fine bathe and went out miles, but the tide was turning so we began to come in. Payne stayed out there. After about five minutes, I turned round and saw that Payne went under at every wave and was spluttering. At first I thought he was pretending to drown, and so I took no notice. A few minutes later, he was still doing it, but in a more panic-stricken way, so I shouted 'What's the matter, Payne, are you fudging?' He didn't answer, but began screaming; so I swam full speed out towards him and caught hold of his arm, and he clambered onto my neck, so that I swam back to shore towing young Payne.

XVIII Winchester Cathedral Choir at Corbière lighthouse, during the visit to the Channel Islands. 28 July 1935

XIX Ready for the early morning shower, summer 1937

XX Easter term 1939. Fancy dress at the Stamp Club Gala in the newly restored 'Priory Room'

In spite of these excitements, the Choir arrived back in Guernsey in time for Evensong at the Town Church. The concert the following afternoon was better received than in Jersey. 'We were clapped very heartily, I am pleased to say, and the concert was a great success. Guernsey people are noted for taking music very seriously.'

There was a last Evensong later in the day, and the Choir left for England next morning. On the way home, Choristers and Lay Clerks gave a short concert on the luggage hatch of the steamer *Isle of Jersey* and, as Humphrey Salwey remembers, 'when sailing up the Solent, we enjoyed seeing King George V racing in his yacht *Britannia*'.

By way of post-script, it should be said that Payne's experience did not deter him from swimming: indeed, before he left the school, he had obtained a first-class swimming certificate. Nevertheless, Dean Selwyn took the precaution, before the second choir trip to the Channel Islands, 14 years later, of drawing up a table of fines ranging from 'for being late: 6d' to 'for being drowned: £5'.

In his editorial to the 1936 *Magazine*, the Headmaster reviewed the progress of the previous five years. The school had grown, and in 1935 a new form had been created in the care of Miss Nancy White (now Mrs. Howard Bostock): the total number of boys was within sight of the target of 56 which was felt to be a comfortable maximum.

'We have thirty more boys in the School now than in 1931', the editorial continued, 'but numbers alone are not enough, nor scholastic or athletic achievements: it is by its old boys that a school should be judged'. Alluding to the important rôle of the preparatory school at a boy's most impressionable age, the Headmaster affirmed: 'It is our aim, in close conjunction with the boys' parents, to lay foundations which will last a life-time'.

As we have seen, the boys of The Pilgrims' School were beginning to achieve success both in the examination room and on the games field. At the same time, new opportunities were being created within the school for their particular interests to be encouraged or awakened.

For example, in the Easter term of 1935, Mr. Phipps formed the Stamp Society, whose double aims were to create a School stamp collection of recent British Empire issues and to encourage and assist boys in forming their own collections. A parent, Mrs. Farley, presented the school with an album and various items of philatelic equipment, and from that moment the Society flourished. Meetings were held three times a term, and every third Saturday Vincent Phipps organised an auction, to allow members to dispose of surplus stock. In March 1937 the members enjoyed the first 'Fancy Dress Gala' with prizes awarded for the best costume. Although entirely unrelated to philatelic matters, this Gala became an indispensable annual fixture, surviving the secretariat of various masters – Anthony Cussans, Herbert Smith, Rodney Blake and Frank Skipwith – until the Sixties. The Stamp Club was revived by the present Headmaster, Michael Kefford, and is now an important out-of-school activity.

Gardening, too, remains a popular activity, even though today's impatient young horticulturalists seldom seem aware that successful gardening projects require long-term planning: the enthusiastic plantings of mid-June scarcely ever reach their best before the summer holidays, and are a tangled wilderness by the autumn. Boys' gardens are first mentioned in the *Magazine* of 1935; prizes were awarded for the six best plots. The following year, the yard of the Dome Alley schoolrooms was grassed over as a practice ground for football, but space was left for 12 large gardens for the boys, thus reviving a custom of the previous Choir School. Gardening was actually timetabled for the junior form of Miss White, IVb, as part of their 'Nature Studies'.

It was Miss Nancy White who was responsible for the encouragement of 'Handicraft', which became a definite part of the school curriculum in September 1935. The first Handicraft Exhibition was held the following March, in 'Dorm I' and the Senior Classroom, and more than 300 parents and friends walked past the displays of paintings, basket-work and modelling. A similar exhibition was held just over a year later, and again in 1939, in the newly-acquired Priory Room.

Meanwhile, the Choristers were given the opportunity of demonstrating their dramatic talent in a performance of *The Children of the Chapel* by Sidney Nicholson, an operetta portraying the re-establishment of the choir of the Chapel Royal following the Restoration of Charles II. This was produced by Miss Cecilia Portal, with the assistance of the Precentor, the Revd. J. G. Hetherington, who accompanied and conducted the last two performances, Harold Rhodes being unwell. The operetta was staged in the St Maurice Hall in Colebrook Street, at the very beginning of January 1936, and preparations kept the Choristers fully occupied during the Christmas 'choir-time'. The cast included Herbert Smith, the Lay Clerk in charge of Choristers, who shortly afterwards became a part-time music teacher at the school. The performance of Anthony Caesar as John Blow was specially commended in the review which Harold Rhodes composed for the *Magazine*.

At the same time as the football ground was established in Dome Alley, the cricket pitch at Wolvesey was enlarged somewhat by levelling and re-turfing the northern end, near to the fence of Bailey's nursery garden. Four cricket nets were put up on a new lawn beside the path leading from the school to the 'Garden Gate', on the spot previously occupied by a venerable mulberry tree reputed to have been planted by Charles II.

The 1936 number of the *Magazine* contained the first report from the Master of the cargo ship S.S. *Canford Chine*, to which the school had become affiliated following an Easter term lecture by a director of the City of London Shipping Company. Inevitably, this interesting link was broken at the outbreak of War. Another account of foreign parts was provided by Mrs. Salwey's brother, then Captain N. F. Penruddocke, who retailed his journey by air from Croydon to Khartoum, while rather nearer home, Tom Scott contributed an article relating his week-long stay on a sail-training ship in Portsmouth harbour with eight Pilgrims' boys.

This venture, the precursor of 'Cruises', 'Ski Trips', 'Brecon Beacons weeks' and the like, was to be Tom Scott's last contribution to the life of the school: he returned to his *alma mater*, Berkhampstead, the following term, though maintaining close links with the preparatory school in which he had played such an active part. Neville Ollerenshaw retains grateful memories of the man 'who gave me my love of History', while Anthony Caesar recalls his instruction in French pronunciation: 'shape your lips to whistle *God Save the King* and then say "tu" '.

Tom Scott was replaced by Hugh Mears Gardner, who taught at The Pilgrims' School for 36 years, with the exception of four years' War service, and became the Set Master of the Monks, proudly wearing his black tie, the Monks' colour, on Mondays, his Set's 'duty day'. 'He seemed more able to come down to our level', commented one old boy. Mr. Gardner introduced Rugger to the school and raised the standard of shooting; he ran the Library in succession to Tom Scott; but above all, he taught French methodically and patiently and is remembered with gratitude by generations of pupils.

'H.M.G.' was soon drafted in to help with extra-curricular activities, not the least of which were the Guy Fawkes celebrations, such a popular annual event before the War. The boys were allowed to buy a small number of fireworks which they would let off in a large circle on Wolvesey playing field. Mr. Payton recalled that one boy bought considerably more than the permitted shilling's-worth, but was punished by fate for his extravagance when 'a sparkler accidentally fell into the box, and the lot went up!'. Vincent Phipps, assisted by Tom Scott and later by Mr. Gardner, was responsible for producing original and ingenious centre-pieces for these displays. One year the Guy arrived in a fiery car; the following November a 20-foot dragon made its appearance; while in 1937 a *Bos longifrons*, pyrotechnic descendent of the creature whose bones had been exhumed in the New Wing excavation, 'suddenly trotted up to the Bonfire and performed circus-tricks among the spectators. Rumour has it that Mr. Phipps was "to the fore" in each of these surprises'.

A few weeks later, in December 1936, two performances of the School Concert were given in the School Hall, formed by opening up the folding doors between the dining room and the Junior Classroom. As the Headmaster recollected years later: 'It was easy enough to push the desks out into the other classroom and send the entire school over to the Cathedral to fetch nearly three hundred chairs. It was very much more difficult to make room for those chairs by passing the heavy dining room tables out of the window into the garden and covering them up if it rained'. In 1936, the whole operation had to be carried out twice, so great was the demand for seats! The concerts ended with a performance of Walford Davies' anthem *God be in my Head* sung by the whole school, an item which concluded all future school concerts during the Headmastership of Humphrey Salwey.

Just as Mr. Payton had introduced hockey into the school in 1936, so the following January Mr. Gardner brought both enthusiasm and skill in rugby football, which provided an alternative Easter term sport for boys to play on three games afternoons a week. The new sport took place on the Winchester RUFC ground, a meadow at Kings Worthy belonging to Mr. Rayson, a racing stable owner. As the Headmaster wryly commented later: 'If only I had known that one of the horses in that paddock was going to win the Derby, how well I should have recompensed myself for shooing those horses away, and doing the necessary "tidying-up" before we started to play!'. Towards the end of the War it proved impossible to get to the Kings Worthy ground, and rugger was played instead on the King Alfred's College pitch at Bar End, or on the adjoining Army playing field, which showed an annoying propensity to flood during the winter. Only from 1967 was it possible to play rugger nearer home, when the Winchester College authorities allowed Pilgrims' to use their 'Palmer Field'. 'New Piece', used by the school since 1966, now also serves as a second, rather small, rugger pitch.

The Easter term of 1936 also saw the introduction of the Railway Club, whose O-gauge lay-out was installed in the attic room now used as 'Dorm IV'. Pilgrims' boys of that generation were confirmed railway enthusiasts, and were encouraged in their passion by the Headmaster, who had once considered joining a railway company before his teaching days began! Mr. Salwey had taken the Choristers on an expedition to Eastleigh locomotive and carriage shops in 1932, and to Basingstoke signal box the following year. He had himself lectured to the school on 'The London Underground', and invited visiting speakers to talk about the Southern Railway and other allied subjects.

The original school lay-out, in tin-plate, was re-laid in 'Millbro' steel track in 1939, and is described in the *Magazine*: 'Double track for most of the way, it runs from Liverpool to Holyhead or London, and from London to Southampton. All four Railways are represented, Liverpool being the HQ of the LMS and LNER, London the SR; while New Winton is the centre for the GWR. Seven boys are required to run a full service of trains, and there are usually about thirty-five members of the Railway Club. Measurements: main-line double track: 91 ft; main-line single track: 54 ft; total length of lines reduced to single track (including sidings): 701 ft. There are seventeen points, nine parallel points, eight cross-overs and two double junctions.'

What a price such a lay-out would realise today, when O-gauge enthusiasts scour the auction rooms in search of equipment! Alas! it was sold in 1967 in favour of a double-O gauge electric system.

During the years immediately before the War, the Dean and Chapter undertook a number of costly projects in the Cathedral. In August 1936 the bells were lowered onto the Quire pavement through a circular panel in the wooden vaulting below the tower, and were taken away to be re-cast. Thus it was that the following February the school was treated to the unforgettable sight of the bells lined up in an imposing semi-circle on the dais for a photograph, before being hoisted up into their belfry again.

Three months later, in June 1937, the famous organ installed for S. S. Wesley was dismantled for restoration. The console was moved from under the organ-pipes to the west end of the 'Ladies' Gallery', and electric action replaced the pneumatic action of 'Father' Willis.

'Owing to the new position of the console', Dr. Rhodes explained, 'the player will, for the first time, be able to hear the organ as it is heard by the congregation. In the past, the balance of tone between voices and organ has been a matter of guesswork to the organist'.

Anthony Caesar remembers the year vividly. 'The Organ was rebuilt in 1937–8 to the great excitement of organ-minded choristers who were treated with consider-able patience and courtesy by Harrison and Harrison's fine craftsmen. We were even allowed to make our way on all fours through the bottom C pipe of the 32-foot open wood while it lay on its side in the North Transept.'

Anthony Cussans recalls that when the organ was being rebuilt, major services (in the Quire) were accompanied by Dr. Rhodes on a concert grand piano, but the everyday services of Mattins and Evensong were held in the Lady Chapel by candlelight, and Harold Rhodes then played a harpsichord. 'There was a real magic about those Evensongs. The long walk up in semi-darkness and then the sweep round past the two chantries, under the brass chandelier (lit again by candles) and so into the Lady Chapel, dim and emotive and very beautiful. I always felt that the atmosphere was medieval and that the ghosts of the Benedictine monks were hovering in the shadows. Some people were a bit scared by it: I revelled in it! And of course, the music had to be chosen with great care, as there was only the harpsichord to accompany us. Therefore, it tended to be all the best of early music: Byrd, Tallis, Gibbons, Wise and their contemporaries. Gorgeous.'

In spite of these expensive ventures, the Dean and Chapter continued to finance the expansion of school facilities, an expansion which more than kept pace with the slowly-increasing school population. Indeed, by 1938 the school had reached its revised maximum of 60 boys, and the Headmaster informed parents that 'We have no intention of increasing our numbers beyond the present point'. The Headmaster of the College, Mr. Spencer Leeson, was but one of several advisors who agreed with Mr. and Mrs. Salwey that 'the school should be a large family'. In fact, the changing circumstances of the War did bring about a modest increase in numbers during the next 10 years, to above 70 boys. In 1951 there was a further increase to an average of 77, but these increases were insignificant compared with the population explosion which followed Humphrey Salwey's retirement as Headmaster. The steady growth in early years was carefully planned and caused no serious overcrowding.

During the Easter holidays of 1938 the boys' changing room was enlarged, with the addition of an extension containing a large footbath and double shower. The following term, four asphalt cricket nets were laid at Blackbridge Yard, the College builders' yard east of New Piece. These nets, installed at the suggestion of Harry Altham, remained in use until the summer of 1966, when they were replaced by similar hard nets in the Dean's garden.

However, the most important addition to the school's facilities took place in 1938, when the Dean and Chapter decided to allow The Pilgrims' School to take over the Priory Stable block for its own use, and devoted part of Miss Pamplin's considerable legacy towards the restoration of the southern part of the building.

The plans for the use of the Priory Stabling were outlined in the 1938 *Magazine*. It seems that at that time there was no immediate intention to displace the Cathedral builders' yard, which had become established in the stable yard and comprised several of the ground-floor rooms at the northern end of the stable block. The proposal was gradually to take over, as further funds became available, the whole of the upper floor of the building and half the ground floor. 'On the right hand side of the entrance, there will be a small classroom [the present Music Room] and space for storing cricket nets and so on. An oak staircase will lead to a playroom, beyond which will be a handicraft room, and further on again, a classroom. At the top of the staircase, there will one day be accommodation for another master.'

Work began on the large room in August 1938, and the 'Priory Room' was opened in December, when a second Handicrafts exhibition allowed parents to see the addition to the school premises. The limited funds did not permit the restoration of the upper floor to proceed further, but the generous donations of parents to the Headmaster's 'Discretionary Fund' were used to create the ground-floor classroom, which was taken over by the junior form, IVb, liberating the Library somewhat, though this had still to double as a handicrafts room.

The large L-shaped room to the right of the new classroom, and running behind it, now the Technology Centre, was ready to store cricket nets, goal posts and other items of sports equipment by the summer term of 1939, but suffered from a grave disadvantage: the wall at right-angles to the stable block, which divided the builders' yard from the 'yard' of The Pilgrims' School, ended so close to the double doors that it was impossible to manoeuvre long objects into the building, or even the trolley which was used to wheel teas down to the Wolvesey field during cricket matches. The Headmaster tried in vain to persuade the Cathedral authorities to reduce the length of the wall by the necessary three feet.

Finally, one dark night I went down with a master and we demolished the necessary amount of that wall, which crumbled away easily in our hands, the mortar being just dust. Now we knew that the Dean kept his car in the shed in the builders' yard; but days went by and he didn't say anything. About a fortnight later, I went to lock my front door, and found a note in the letter-box, addressed to me. There was no signature, but I recognised the writing. It was typical of the Dean's sense of humour: a sentence from the Commination service: 'Cursed be he that removeth his neighbour's landmark!'.

And so the summer term of 1939 drew to an end. There was an open-air performance of Euripides' *Medea* in the grounds of Winchester College, and a madrigal and orchestral concert in the Deanery garden, at which 16 senior Pilgrims acted as lamp-lighters, lighting no fewer than 500 candle lanterns! Two days before the end of term, Dean Selwyn presented the prizes and congratulated the school on the successes of the past year. Perhaps it was preferable to look back; for six weeks later, Britain was at war.

Chapter Six

THE SECOND WORLD WAR

AS EUROPE moved inevitably towards a state of war, the staff of The Pilgrims' School were on holiday, widely scattered both in England and abroad. Mr. and Mrs. Salwey were staying in Brittany with their son Michael. Mr. Gardner was in the Jura mountains. Yet the day after war was declared, all assembled at the school, on 4 September 1939, to discuss the implications of the previous day's events, and make plans for the future.

Term started as arranged, on 22 September, and only two boys were prevented from rejoining the school. There was one immediate change on the staff: Miss Nancy White, who had already handed over her junior form to Miss Marsham but had stayed on to help with handicrafts, now joined a mobile V.A.D. unit, and Miss Marsham took over the rest of her work.

The Dean and Chapter had already made provisions for residents of the Cathedral Close, including The Pilgrims' School and the Atherley School for Girls, which had been evacuated from Southampton to Winchester, to use the Cathedral crypt as an air-raid shelter if necessary. The drawback was obvious: hardly a winter passes without the crypt flooding with the rise in the water-table. So, in the summer of 1939, a huge platform was erected in the crypt so that would-be shelterers could keep their feet dry during the winter months!

As the War progressed, some preparatory schools in Winchester began to evacuate to safer parts of Britain: West Downs moved to Blair Atholl Castle, in Scotland; West Hayes to the Lake District; and Winton House to the Midlands. The question of the possible evacuation of The Pilgrims' School was brought up, and Humphrey and Lorna Salwey were dispatched to examine the possibility of moving the school to an empty property belonging to the Salwey family – Moor Park, at Richard's Castle, near Ludlow. However it became clear that too much would have to be done to the house to make it suitable for a school premises, and it was unanimously resolved that the school should stay in Winchester Cathedral Close where it belonged.

The Salweys felt that it was hardly practicable for boys to use the crypt as a night-time shelter, and made their own arrangements. It was of course not feasible to dig an underground shelter in this low-lying part of Winchester: such an excavation would quickly have filled with water. However, it was possible to modify the basement corridor and cellarage of the school by installing stout timber shoring along the corridor so that boys could, if needs be, take refuge in a relatively safe part of the school buildings: safe, that is, except in the event of a direct hit.

The Dean was not impressed by these arrangements, and a protracted argument developed. Eventually, Humphrey and Lorna Salwey wrote to all the parents, seeking their authorisation to leave all the boys in bed unless Winchester was in actual danger.

Every single parent entirely agreed with us. Shortly afterwards, I was invited to see Spencer Leeson, the College Headmaster: he pointed out that I was up against the Dean and Chapter and asked me what I was going to do. So I produced the pile of replies from the parents, having been careful to put on top the one signed by Lord Mottistone who had a grandson in the school. Spencer Leeson took one look at the pile and said, 'I will write a *précis* of our conversation and pass it on to the Dean and Chapter'. And that was the end of the affair.

During the 'Phoney War' school life continued much as before. There were the usual lectures: Miss Newbury returned to talk on 'Albania' and Mr. H. G. Davis on the 'Romance of Railway Transport'. Mr. Gardner developed his scheme to encourage artistic appreciation by displaying reproductions of famous pictures in the dining room and Junior Classroom. Boys were put in charge of changing these pictures from time to time, and writing a note on the painting and its artist.

There were innovations, like the miniature racing track for 'Minic' cars established by Messrs. Phipps and Gardner, who periodically acted as Race Marshals. 'The first meeting on 21 October consisted of three races, but later on the track was improved and there were as many as 112 starters in nine events.' There was a change from rugger and hockey during the bitterly cold winter of 1939–40, when skating and tobogganing replaced more traditional games until the end of February.

Some events suffered, however. There could be no Guy Fawkes celebrations, and the Carol Service had to be cancelled because of black-out regulations. This was particularly unfortunate because the previous year there had been no Christmas service either, when the boys of the Choir had gone down with chicken-pox and all choir-time arrangements had been cancelled.

The effects of the War gradually became more pronounced. In 1940, The Pilgrims' School became an Air Raid Precautions Post, 'Post 18', covering the Close and Wolvesey: Mr. Salwey was Senior Warden. Mr. Payton combined the duties of Air Raid Warden and Home Guard, while Mr. Gardner was put in charge of a section of the Auxiliary Fire Service, and looked after a fire-engine kept in the garage in the Cathedral builders' yard.

The log book recording the activities of 'Post 18' has survived, and the first entries describe the prelude to Hitler's planned invasion of the British Isles, 'Operation Sealion'. The air-raid sirens sounded during the early hours of three nights in June; little was observed, though Warden Salwey noted that 'on each occasion the two services (A.R.P. and A.F.S.) have been on parade remarkably quickly'. Then, in mid-August, Goering intensified his daylight raids:

August 13th 1940: Warning 3.45 – 5.10 p.m. Payton away on holiday, otherwise all present. Heavy machine-gun fire and 'diving' in the clouds over Eastleigh. Two bullets picked up by Kingsgate archway.

August 15th 1940: 5.43 – 6.15 p.m. Air battle overhead. Parachute down, Hursley way. Saw German bomber on the ground, North of Twyford.

The day of the Luftwaffe's most concentrated daylight raid, and the climax of the Battle of Britain, 15 September, seems to have been quite peaceful in Winchester. The only entry reads:

Sept 15th 1940: 5.50 – 6.10 p.m. 12 German fighters went over St Swithun's School.

A few days earlier The Pilgrims' School's first war victim had died. F. P. H. Stuttaford had been in a Brighton cinema, arranging a charity performance for schoolchildren, when the building was bombed; both he and the manager were killed.

After the Battle of Britain, Goering switched to night-time attacks, and the entries in the Log of 'Post 18' become more frequent, though less detailed. One further daylight bombing raid on Southampton is recorded, when games were stopped but 'we carried on changing and went into school in the main building'. From November 1940 until the following May the alert was sounded virtually every night, and the log book provides a record of the numbers entertained after the 'all clear' had been heard. 'Mrs. Salwey's 2 a.m. tea parties in the kitchen became quite an institution', wrote the Headmaster later. 'On some occasions as many as twenty-eight men and women came in for refreshment.'

At this time Lorna Salwey's domestic staff was reduced to a cook and two helpers, while the burden of ration books and coupons added greatly to her responsibilities.

During 287 'alerts' totalling 480 hours, the boys needed to be brought down from their dormitories only three times.

And I well remember the first occasion. I rushed into the junior dormitory and told them to come down. Then I went round the other dormitories: and when I returned to the juniors, who were drunk with sleep, one was saying his prayers, another had gone to brush his teeth and the others had got back into bed!

John Maynard recalls one of those occasions. 'A frankly terrifying night, when bombs on Bushfield Camp caused the Cathedral bells to vibrate and produce a chilling noise.' But on other occasions, 'when the reverberation of bombs and our own heavy gunfire caused the bells to hum and the rattle of the Deanery letter-box to echo round the Close, many boys slept blissfully through everything'.

In fact Winchester escaped lightly during the Blitz unlike, for example, Coventry where Dr. Rhodes had formerly been organist; he was heart-broken when the cathedral there was destroyed by enemy action. For some reason Winchester was excluded from the 'Baedeker raids' which hit Exeter, Norwich, Canterbury and other cathedral towns so heavily. Perhaps the proximity of Southampton, a priority target, saved the City, though a legend grew up among local primary-school children that the Luftwaffe had been told not to bomb Winchester because 'Adolf Hitler wanted to be crowned King of England in Winchester Cathedral'!

Winchester was bombed just once. On the morning of 9 February 1943, a raider came out of the clouds and dropped a stick of six bombs from the corner of North Walls and Hyde Street to Kings Worthy. Six people who happened to be waiting for a 'bus in Hyde Street were killed instantly, and one of several wounded died later. John Maynard was on his way to the Dome Alley classrooms when this raid occurred:

> One wet morning, we were preparing to cross the Close to Dome Alley when there was a very loud aircraft noise. Through the low cloud appeared a Dornier 217, which unloaded two or three bombs on Winchester. I was beside myself with excitement, but less happy to collect a monumental rocket from Mr. Salwey for being idiot enough to stand there watching.

As the War developed, there were several staff changes. In August 1940, Vincent Phipps obtained a commission with the Coldstream Guards. This was the end of his successful career as a schoolmaster, for after the War he went into the insurance business, travelling to Kenya and Venezuela. When he retired to Ringwood, he set up a business which, in memory of his first job, he named 'Pilgrims Caravans'.

The following term, the number of boys in the school had risen to 67, and it was decided to create a new form called the 'Remove'. Thus C. G. Fitzmaurice was appointed as an additional member of the staff. He had formerly taught at West Hayes, a local preparatory school. 'Fitz' was the first Set Master of the 'Saxons', named after the builders of Winchester's Old Minster. He taught a number of subjects, but perhaps excelled in the coaching of games: he took charge of swimming and after the War was the driving force behind the school's tennis court. Not the least of his contributions towards the life of the school was the careful preparation of the field at Wolvesey for the School Sports, year by year.

Mrs. Aileen Emmet also joined the staff in January 1941, replacing Miss Marsham, who had married. Mrs. Emmet was the wife of a College 'don', and like her predecessor she possessed the happy gift of encouraging the less academically inclined. Towards the end of the War, Humphrey Salwey was astonished to discover her coaching her nephew for the Eton Election Greek paper!

During his time in the Fire Service, Mr. Gardner had been kept busy in Southampton and Plymouth, and John Maynard remembers him 'returning from the Southampton Blitz with his hands cut, blistered and bandaged'. In 1942 he joined R.A.F. India Command, and was replaced during his four years abroad by George Heathcote, scion of an old Hampshire family from Hursley. In January the following year, Miss D. Goodman Harvey began her long association with the school, taking the boys for drawing and teaching one of the junior forms.

There were changes at Winchester College. Mr. Gear came out of retirement, when his successor as P.T. Instructor, Sergeant-Major Reid, was recalled to the Scots Guards; and the school's carpentry instructor, Mr. Savage, rejoined the Royal Engineers. Thus it was that the College carpentry instructor, Mr. Laverty, began instructing Pilgrims' boys. He was successful in obtaining supplies of materials throughout the difficult war years, and generated tremendous interest.

In 1943 half the school took carpentry lessons, the main exception being the Choristers, whose commitments in the Cathedral rather precluded such outside activities.

Music was probably less affected by the War. There was as yet no permanent music teacher on the staff, but Dr. Rhodes was in charge of the school's music, ably helped by the Assistant Organist, Dr. Fogwell, the Lay Clerk, Mr. Herbert Smith, and Miss Fulcher, who taught the violin from the early years of the War until the mid-Sixties.

A School Concert, given on two evenings at the end of March 1941, included the first performance of the *Pilgrims' School Song*, written by the Dean and set to music by Harold Rhodes. There are references to the four Sets then in existence, and to various extra-curricular activities: the lectures ('showing as in magic lens, all that's writ on History's page'), the Stamp and Railway Clubs ('Who's for philatelic lore, Who's for trains and railway lines?'), and perhaps an allusion to the War itself ('Though the darkness round us drifts'). Although circumstances and pastimes have changed, the stirring tune and optimistic words have assured the survival of the Song, which is sung by the boys at the end of every term (after the staff have left the room – an inexplicable custom!).

Another expression of optimism involved the official life of the Cathedral. Just as the Cathedral Statutes of Henry VIII, revised under Charles I, had made provision for the education of the Cathedral Choristers, so the revised Statutes of 1942 specifically recognised The Pilgrims' School as the foundation created for this purpose.

Provision for the general education of the Choristers was made as follows: 'So that in learning they fall not behind other boys of like age and standing, the Dean and Chapter shall maintain to that purpose the Pilgrims' School in the Close, and shall choose a Schoolmaster for it, one of honest repute and uncorrupt life, moreover distinguished by a title of learning, who shall teach the boys and imbue them with modesty of manners'.

Successive years of bad weather (1940), chicken-pox (1941), illness in other schools (1941–42) and measles (1942–43) proved more effective than Herr Hitler in preventing competitive sport against neighbouring teams. However, from 1943 it was impossible to reach the Kings Worthy rugby ground with ease as coaches were no longer available, and the Bar End sports field leased by the Army was used instead. Food rationing had its effect on sport too: the lavish pre-war cricket teas were reduced to tea and biscuits, while cash prizes replaced chocolate in 'Bowling for the Plate'.

In the face of such privations, flowers naturally gave way to vegetables in the boys' gardens, just as they had done at Colebrook House 25 years previously.

The 'dig for Victory' campaign fired our budding gardeners with enthusiasm and there was a steady demand for ground space. Quite a large area in Dome Alley was dug up and planted with an assortment of vegetables. Only a very few flowers were to be seen; and apart from potatoes, the choice was especially lettuces, together with radishes, cress and so on.

The war-time *School Magazines* also record the sad deterioration of the Railway

Club's equipment. By 1943 a large number of engines were in need of overhaul; before the end of the War there were no locomotives left, and only fortunate private owners were able to use the school lay-out. Not until the early Fifties was it possible to replace the broken springs and revive one of the most popular pre-war activities.

However, other clubs were formed which did not need such delicate equipment. One of these was the 'Spotters' Club' founded in the winter of 1942 by two young aviation enthusiasts, John Maynard and Bill Everett. In this venture they enlisted the support of Herbert Smith, who had joined the Observers Corps: indeed, Mr. Smith seems to have been the inspiration behind the Club. 'I remember Mr. Smith', recalls John Maynard, 'who failed to teach me music, but inspired me by showing me a first picture of a Mosquito, and warning me that he faced a long stretch in the Tower for doing so.'

The Club met weekly, and produced a fortnightly magazine known as *The Cloud*. 'The magazine was hand written and illustrated with drawings and paintings. I remember that one of our "scoops" was the first big Lancaster raid on Augsburg, following which Squadron Leader Nettleton was awarded the V.C. We wrote about the raid with a measure of journalistic licence and persuaded an old boy living in Winchester to draw a portrait of Nettleton which we stuck in with enormous care: photographs were not considered suitable for publication.'

Such was the beginning of John Maynard's life-time interest in flying, including 20 years in the aircraft industry. The 'Spotters' Club' naturally came to an end with the defeat of Germany.

Equally ephemeral was 'The Pilgrims' School Broadcasting Corporation', brain-child of M. Cole (chief engineer, head announcer and general inspiration), whose team broadcast week-end programmes from the dining hall to the Priory Room. At about the same time, Cole's father presented the school with an early item of audio hardware: a loudspeaker, which enabled radio broadcasts to be relayed from the Headmaster's study to the Senior Classroom.

Much more important, in view of its subsequent development, was the Music Club, founded in February 1942 by Anthony Cussans, an old boy of the school, who joined the staff for a short but influential year between King's School, Canterbury, and the Rifle Brigade. The present tradition of Commoner music began with this small group of enthusiasts, limited at first to 20 members. Dr. Rhodes was elected President at the first meeting and spoke on 'The Composition of an Orchestra', and from then on meetings took place regularly on Saturday evenings, when members listened to lectures or gramophone records, occasionally attending outside orchestral or choral concerts, mainly in the Cathedral. The earliest activities of the Music Club are well documented in the surviving Minute Books, which contain critical comments by the boy secretary, such as 'The pro-gramme consisted of Litolf's *Concerto Symphonique* which, for all its faulty orches-tration, none of us could help liking'!

Anthony Cussans also revived the Stamp Society and, during the summer term, the 'Model Yacht Club', which had originally been created during his time at the school as a Chorister. 'It was given the grandiose name of the Itchen Yacht Club', he recalls. 'It had its own burgee and flag-staff and was "officially" inaugurated in the summer of 1942 by Captain Vincent Phipps, Coldstream Guards.' Meetings were held every Saturday evening on the stretch of river at the end of the garden.

The final Regatta, in July, was attended by Mr. Justice Charles and a colleague, Mr. Justice Lawrence, who was later to play a prominent part in the Nuremburg Trials.

Anthony Cussans was also responsible for encouraging the collection of public school shields in the boys' entrance hall.

> Heraldry was (and still is) my great interest; and I designed – most illegally – The Pilgrims' School arms with the saltire (Salwey) and the pilgrims' shells. It is OK heraldically, but not "granted" to the school by the College of Arms.

In 1942 the Winchester College Head of Science, Dr. Humby, visited the school and was agreeably surprised to learn that the Pilgrims' curriculum did not consist entirely of Classics as he had assumed. He was impressed by the Mathematics teaching, but complained nevertheless that 'prep-school boys knew no science': he was compelled to start from scratch. As a result of his suggestions, the Science Club came into being, under the guidance of Mr. Payton. From these humble beginnings developed one of the school's most flourishing departments. At first, the Club's activities were restricted by a lack of facilities: it was imposssible to equip a laboratory during the War.

The Choir's activities continued relatively unhampered by war-time restrictions. The black-out regulations caused some difficulty however. The 6.30 Sunday Parish Evensong was abandoned during the winter months and was eventually discontinued altogether. The Carol Service was revived in 1940, on the other hand, by the simple expedient of holding it during daylight hours; and thus it continued until 1944 when 'dim-out' replaced 'black-out' and it was possible to hold the service in the evening once again. That Christmas the Carol Service was attended by large numbers of American soldiers. The Band of the U.S. Army gave their own carol concert in the Cathedral a few days later, on New Year's Eve, and invited the Choristers to a Christmas party, where they were supplied with unwholesome quantities of candy. But for some of the Choristers, their own service was particularly moving and memorable because of the groups of German prisoners, clearly overwhelmed by proceedings, who had been brought in from their P.O.W. camp at Micheldever.

The Choir gave a number of broadcasts during the War: Evensong was broadcast on the Home Service in 1943 and 1944, and recordings were made for transmission on the Overseas Service. In this way Winchester Cathedral played its part in boosting national morale.

The Dean and Mrs. Selwyn showed their gratitude by reviving the Turkey Feast in 1942, despite the problems of rationing, and during the later War years, Mrs. Selwyn and the Salweys performed the apparently impossible, providing strawberry or raspberry teas after the annual cricket match between the Choristers and the Dean and Chapter.

It was during one school cricket match in May 1944, as Andrew Maynard recalls, that 'apparently half the American Eighth Air Force appeared in a mass of condensation trails over the northern horizon and droned across a clear blue sky heading out over Southampton. Cricket had never held too much for me, and the number of balls that went past me in the deep field that day confirmed Mr. Payton's long-held belief that he hadn't got a Denis Compton on his hands'.

That July the anti-tank defences at the entrance to Wolvesey and in Kingsgate Street were demolished, a sign that the War was at last drawing to its close. Ten months later, Germany capitulated.

V.E. Day, 8 May 1945, was celebrated as a whole holiday. Some boys were able to go out with parents or friends, and others went to the cinema, but at 9.00 p.m. all listened to the King's broadcast. Later that evening, all but the most junior boys climbed the Cathedral Tower to see the bonfires on St Catherine's Hill and beyond. On 17 May members of the school attended the Victory March at the Guildhall, where they watched the Lord-Lieutenant of Hampshire, Lord Mottistone, take the salute. Shortly afterwards, the school received another distinguished visitor, as Humphrey Salwey relates:

> About thirteen days after the end of the War in Europe, I was rung up by Mrs. Spencer Leeson to say that 'Monty' was about to come to talk to the College men: would we like him to come round and meet our boys when he'd finished with them? I said 'yes' of course, and in due course Field Marshal Montgomery arrived, with a police escort. We had the entire school assembled together, including the domestic staff: I introduced the teaching staff to him, and he then went in to speak to the school.

Addressing the boys in the dining hall, 'Monty' referred to the problems facing him in conquered Germany, and urged the boys 'to make the most of every opportunity to prepare themselves for the problems that lay ahead'.

Thus the War ended. On 15 August, Humphrey Salwey sat down to write an editorial for the *Magazine*: 'Many thoughts surge through our mind on this day, when the submission of Japan has been announced. Among the foremost are naturally those of thankfulness and relief, mingled with gratitude to those who, in their different ways, have done so much to achieve this end.'

In a brief review of the years of conflict, the Headmaster alluded to the difficulties that had faced the school, and Mrs. Salwey and her devoted team of domestic staff in particular. Despite everything, academic standards had continued to rise: of 73 boys who left during the War, 33 had been awarded scholarships or exhibitions, and the others had passed happily into their Public Schools. Encouraged by these continued successes, the school should now look to the future.

Chapter Seven

INTO THE FIFTIES

AS EUROPE returned to peace, it became possible for the school to renew its contacts with Old Boys. The Old Boy Club had been renamed 'The Shell' after the symbol used by medieval pilgrims on the road to Santiago, which Anthony Cussans had included on his unofficial school coat of arms. Because of travel restrictions and food rationing, however, it was impossible to arrange a reunion of Old Pilgrims until the end of 1947, when 30 members of The Shell returned to the school. Although a few Old Boys had visited Winchester during the War, contact between members of The Shell had been maintained largely through the columns of the *Magazine*; and the school had acted as a forwarding address for mail between its ex-pupils.

Towards the end of the War, a number of Old Pilgrims had become eligible for active service. As well as the civilian casualty, Stuttaford, two of them had lost their lives in action. Pilot Officer Jack Graham, Bomber Command, had been shot down while returning from a raid on Germany in 1942; and Flight-Lieutenant Stuart Woodhouse was shot down over Northern Italy on 30 August 1943, while on photographic reconnaissance. Six Old Pilgrims had been wounded, including Anthony Cussans and John Hunter, who contributed articles relating their wartime experiences to the *Magazine*; as did Andrew Fairbairn, who had spent seven months in a P.O.W. camp near Hanover, and R. C. Macpherson and Neville Ollerenshaw, who had seen service in the Far East and Egypt respectively.

The end of the War brought some changes on the staff, both full- and part-time. The College P.T. Instructor, Mr. Gear, retired for the second time; and Mr. Savage, who had coached Pilgrims' School boys in carpentry before the War, returned to his old job after four years in a P.O.W. camp. In February 1946 Mr. Gardner was 'demobbed' from the R.A.F. and George Heathcote retired. Mr. Gardner returned just in time for the end of the rugger season; this sport could take place at the Kings Worthy ground once more, now that transport was available. Finally, at the end of 1946, Mrs. Aileen Emmet left the school in order to give full-time assistance to her husband, who was shortly to take over Chernocke House at the College.

Meanwhile, the 25 members of the Music Club had the opportunity of listening to some fine music in the Cathedral. Visiting soloists included the ex-chorister

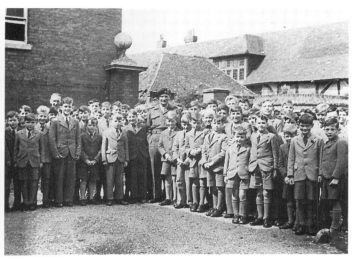

XXI Field Marshal Montgomery
visits the school, May 1945

XXII The Shooting VIII, Easter
term 1946, with H. Mears Gardner,
Michael Salwey and R.S.M. Starr

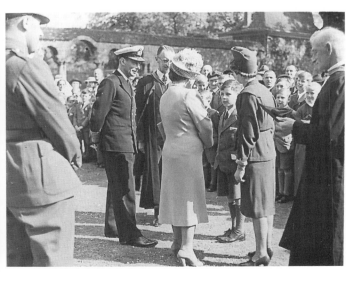

XXIII The Royal Visit, 17 May 1946.
King George VI and Queen Elizabeth
talk to Henry Seymour

Eric Greene, who gave a recital in November 1945 and returned a few weeks later as soloist in Handel's *Messiah*, and Peter Pears, who took the part of the Evangelist in the Winchester Music Club's performance of Bach's *St John Passion* in March 1946, a performance in which the soprano arias were sung by the College Quiristers.

However, the most memorable event of the first few months of peace must surely have been the Royal Visit of King George VI and Queen Elizabeth. After a civic reception in the City, where over a thousand schoolchildren enthusiastically sang the National Anthem in Castle Square, under the direction of the Sub-Organist Dr. Fogwell, the Royal couple visited the Cathedral. They emerged by the south door, to be greeted by those same thousand school children and the boys of The Pilgrims' School. It so happened that the mother of one of the boys, Henry Seymour, was Lady-in-Waiting to the Queen that day, and Her Majesty asked to speak to the boy. Meanwhile, the King was talking with the Headmaster, and asked for an extra week's holiday for the school in honour of the Royal visit.

> And then he suddenly stopped and said, 'I must see what Kate thinks'. I just couldn't think who Kate was! Of course, it was Lady Katherine Seymour. Fortunately she said that she would be delighted to have Henry at home for another week; and so the Dean and Chapter were deprived of their Choristers for a further seven days, that summer!

About three years later, when he was at Eton, Henry Seymour became a Page to Queen Elizabeth, and the Salweys received an invitation to be guests of Their Majesties at the State Opening of Parliament. A happy coincidence made the day even more memorable: it was Humphrey Salwey's 50th birthday.

During the War the number of boys at The Pilgrims' School had increased somewhat. Perhaps the school had expanded at the expense of those preparatory schools which evacuated to safer parts of Britain. By 1943 the total had risen to 69, and it was once again necessary to find accommodation elsewhere in the Close. Mrs. Gordon Selwyn describes how some of the senior Choristers slept at the Deanery:

> Owing to overcrowding at the school, we housed four boys: this was considered something of a treat. My husband used to read to them on Thursday evenings in the Winter: this was very popular, and they sat curled up in front of the fire. He was a beautiful reader, and they used to choose the book that was to be read together.

Anthony Cussans, who in earlier years had boarded in the Deanery, recalls that 'he had a marvellous voice, but we were a little bemused when he read us Greek verse. His comment was "you may not understand this, but just listen to the sound".' The Dean's bedtime stories occasionally caused trouble if the Headmaster discovered that the boys had stayed up after the official 'lights-out' time!

Other senior Choristers lodged at Cheyney Court, and, as ex-Head Chorister Gavin Roynon recollects, 'this gave us early experience of living in rather exalted "digs": it was my lot to share a room with a fellow-Chorister at Cheyney Court for two years. Canon Lloyd was tolerant, so long as we did not disturb him on evenings when he was listening to concerts on the radio. Obviously he felt that Choristers must be warm-blooded fellows, for the room was always at a sub-zero temperature in the winter – and in the freeze-up of 1946–47 I am sure that we had the coldest room in Christendom. As a result we wore most of our clothes in bed at night, as well as during the day!'

Thus it was that Gavin Roynon came to know Canon Lloyd well.

He was a great authority on railways, and was said to have been arrested at the station on one occasion on suspicion of being the Mad Parson, then being sought up and down the length and breadth of the country. When in residence, he frequently left Cheyney Court at the last possible moment before Evensong and could be seen, cassock flying in the wind, sprinting across the Close.

On one occasion George Bryant, Head Virger, was rather late in taking Canon Lloyd up to the lectern at the end of the interminably long Psalm set for the 15th Evening of the month.

'So sorry, Sir', said George after the service. 'I was so engrossed in the Psalm that I entirely forgot to take you up until the Gloria.'

'My dear man', replied Canon Lloyd, 'if you had given me any other excuse than that, I should have forgiven you!'

The demanding life of the Choristers brought them into contact with other members of the Chapter. There was Canon Burrows, the Archdeacon of Winchester, 'a genial character who shone as a useful left-arm bowler in the annual First XI match between the school and the Dean and Chapter'. The Bishop of Southampton, Bishop Morgan, 'sang with great gusto with his spectacles at a bizarre angle up the top of his forehead'. Senior member of the Chapter was Canon Moor, who had been living in the Close from the very earliest days of the school. 'Somewhat intense but most kind and friendly', recalls Anthony Caesar. 'He put great meaning into his reading, giving a characteristic sideways shake of the head at words he wished to emphasise.'

First and foremost was Dean Selwyn. Aristocratic of countenance, dignified, respected by the Choristers but not feared, he took a sincere interest in all the boys at the school he had founded and was never happier than when he had the boys around him. Nevertheless, in the Cathedral he was 'a formidable personality whose word was law'.

The life of the Choristers was enlivened and enriched by daily contact with the Dean and Chapter, Organists, Lay Clerks and Virgers. It was also very demanding, with 11 sung services a week (including two sung Mattins) for 40 weeks in the year, on top of a busy school programme. 'Humphrey Salwey rightly insisted that Choristers should miss no essential work and as few school activities as possible (boxing and carpentry were the only two that I can remember).' In this way the Headmaster safe-guarded against any danger that the Choristers might be seen as the *élite* and the Commoners as second-class citizens. Both sections of the school community gained from each other.

Perhaps the most lasting memories of former Choristers are of Christmas choir-time, when they had the entire school to themselves, under the devoted supervision of the Salweys and the 'Master in Charge of Choir-time' (Mr. Payton, Fitzmaurice or Gardner).

'Thanks to the remarkable kindness and generosity of Humphrey and Lorna Salwey, none of us felt that we were "missing out" by not spending Christmas at home', writes Gavin Roynon.

No part of the traditional Christmas festivities was forgotten, despite post-war shortages and rationing – and Lorna even managed, by dint of brilliant organisation behind the scenes, to ensure that each Chorister received a silver threepenny-bit in his Christmas pudding.

Christmas Day itself was frantically exciting, especially in the early morning, when stockings were being opened. One year, after first Grandorge and then Whitrow (or it may have been the other way round) fainted and had to be carried out from Mattins under the disapproving eye of the Dean, all sweets were banned until after the morning Service.

The two highlights were the annual Turkey Feast and the Carol Service in the Cathedral. The former, which was a Christmas Party held in the Deanery for the Choristers' benefit, started with a splendid meal. But the riotous part of the evening derived from the games which followed, organised by the Dean himself. All the clergy were expected to take part and seemed to enjoy letting their hair down; perhaps it made a welcome break from their spiritual duties. It was certainly a change for these distinguished clerics to charge around the room playing General Post – and I can still remember the consummate skill with which the Bishop of Southampton flapped and flipped his paper fish with a ping-pong bat along the Dean's drawing-room floor to finish the winner – just a short head in front of the Venerable Archdeacon.

If the Turkey Feast was a private occasion, the Carol Service saw the Choir very much in the public eye, with the Cathedral packed. Invariably we felt that this was *the* service of the year and responded with heart and soul to the cajoling and musical expertise of Dr. Rhodes. A pupil of Stanford, Harold Rhodes was a hard but sensitive taskmaster with very high standards. If we hurried *In dulci jubilo* or sang *The Angel Gabriel* (a carol of which he was very fond) without sufficient expression, he would threaten to scrap them. Not a serious threat perhaps, but nothing but the best would do for the Carol Service.

The evening of the Service itself was a magic one, with the full Cathedral poised in silence. Then at a given moment, singing would start near the Sanctuary of St Swithun, Decani and Cantoris would separate down the two aisles either side of the Nave, and the whole Cathedral, lit only by the lanterns of the Choristers and the flashing baton of Dr. Rhodes, echoed and re-echoed to the antiphonal choral rejoicing of Prendergast's *Make we Merry in Hall and Bower* . . . The Choir was re-united under the Christmas Tree at the West End, processed together up the centre of the Nave, and yet another Carol Service was launched after weeks of painstaking preparation and practice.

The year 1947 was a quiet one. There was a school concert, which included some scenes from Shakespeare, loosely linked by additional dialogue and entitled *Such Stuff as Dreams are made on*. In July the school defeated a Dean and Chapter cricket team which included no fewer than three Bishops! A few days later, Mr. Payton arranged a fixture between the First XI and a team of Old Pilgrims at Winchester College. He provided a sumptuous tea by the walls of Wolvesey Castle. Such was his leaving treat to the school, for a few days later he left to take up employment in the North Midlands. This proved to be a short-lived venture, and he was drawn back to The Pilgrims' School two years later.

By this short absence, Mr. Payton missed witnessing the fulfilment of his Science Club's cherished dream. Throughout the War, a wistful paragraph had appeared in the club report, 'one day we hope that it may be possible to equip a small laboratory . . . '. In the Christmas term of 1947 a corner of the Priory stabling was equipped with a bunsen burner and running water. Mr. St John, a master from Peter Symonds' School, who had acted as lecturer and principal adviser to the club, handed over its general running to a colleague, Mr. W. Ferguson, who ran an entertaining course on 'gases'. Early in 1948 several gas-filled balloons were released. One reached Maidstone, and another was found near Charterhouse, appropriately enough, as it had been sent off by Christopher Salwey, who entered that school the following term.

Salwey's co-launcher was R. McLachlan, who shortly afterwards became the second Pilgrim to be placed 'Head of the Roll' in the Winchester College Election, and who later followed a career in theoretical science. The year 1948 was an excellent one for academic successes. Seven scholarships were won altogether, including top awards at Winchester, Radley and Cranleigh. Bryan Salwey obtained a cadetship at Dartmouth.

During the Easter term of 1948 the Shooting Eight won the St David's Shield Competition for the sixth time running. Much of this success must be credited to R.S.M. Starr of Winchester College, who from 1938 had coached the school's 12 best 'shots'. The Salwey's eldest son, Michael, who had achieved considerable success at Bisley two years earlier, had also played an important part in teaching the boys to shoot. In the Easter term of 1947 a shooting team which included both Christopher and Bryan Salwey achieved a score actually higher than the 'Possible' 600 points, after addition of the allowance for the use of open sights. It was an impressive achievement.

There were great changes and developments in 1949. It will be remembered that the northern end of the meadow in front of Wolvesey Palace was occupied by a market garden, which had been run by the same family, Messrs. Bailey, since 1776. In 1949 their lease was about to expire. The Dean and Chapter, supported by the Bishop, Mervyn Haigh, promised the land to The Pilgrims' School for use as an additional playing field, and the new agreement was signed and sealed the following year.

In the same year, the 'Pilgrims' School Society' was created. Two parents, Donald McLachlan and Dr. P. A. T. Lowden were the prime movers in the formation of this body, which was 'to keep in touch with the needs and work of the school, help it with advice, interest and modest financial assistance'. An exploratory letter appeared in the 1949 *Magazine*, and the first meeting was held in the Priory Room on 10 June the following year, when the Constitution and Rules were accepted and the Society officially came into being. Walter Oakeshott, Headmaster of Winchester College, was elected the first President, Geoffrey Crowther, Vice-President, while Vincent Payton took on the task of Secretary. The Committee included three parents, Mrs. Aileen Emmet and the Headmaster. A useful start to the Society's funds was provided by the closure of the 'Headmaster's Discretionary Fund', which was no longer required.

Mr. Payton's return to Winchester was announced in the summer of 1949. He had returned to the school frequently during his exile in the Midlands, and earlier that year had brought a group of boys to the Winchester College Election. During that visit he had invited all Old Pilgrims at the College, and all members of The Pilgrims' staff to dine at the *Royal Hotel*. Perhaps he was encouraged to return by the favourable reports he had heard of sporting successes. The years 1948 and 1949 were unusually free from major illnesses, and the school fielded powerful teams in all major sports, particularly in cricket, where the First XI lost only one of their 10 matches.

That same summer term the Choir paid a second trip to the Channel Islands, then in the grip of a drought. The Choristers were accommodated at Victoria College in St Helier, and all members of the party led by the Dean were entertained at Government House by the Lieutenant Governor. There the Choir gave the first of two concerts consisting mainly of madrigals and secular songs. There were three services in Jersey, and opportunities for bathing – a welcome relief during that exceptional summer – before the Choir moved on to Guernsey, where they took part in similar engagements. There was a trip to Herm, but on this occasion there were no dramatic incidents! A few Choristers were lucky enough to spend an extra few hours in the Channel Islands with the Dean, and visited the island of Sark, where they swam in the natural rock-pool known as the Venus Pool.

This most successful tour was Dr. Rhodes' last engagement with the Choir. He retired as Organist and Master of the Choristers that summer. He had been in charge of the music of Winchester Cathedral for 16 years, and his personal qualities endeared him to all those who had worked with him. The Headmaster received many letters expressing sorrow at Harold Rhodes' departure, and their gratitude for his teaching, kindly training and ability to inspire and foster a true love of music. At a farewell tea-party, the Choristers presented him with a dispatch case, while the Old Choristers subscribed towards a bookcase for his new home in Surrey. In a thank-you letter, Dr. Rhodes wrote

It has been one of the richest joys of my life, and a rare privilege, to take part in training such a splendid body of young men; and I am glad of this opportunity of thanking them for all the loyal support they have given me. The more difficult the task, the more enthusiastic was the response at all times.

Harold Rhodes was succeeded by Mr. Alwyn Surplice from Bristol Cathedral. Mr. Surplice's first services were held in the Nave, because the Quire was filled with scaffolding while the wooden ceiling was cleaned and repaired and the roof bosses painted. He was assisted by a new Sub-Organist, Mr. J. Bennett, for Dr. Fogwell was already suffering from the long illness which finally killed him in the summer of 1950. Alwyn Surplice was immediately elected President of the Pilgrims' School Music Club at its first meeting of the new term, and thus endeared himself to the Commoners of the school, as well as his Choristers.

The early Fifties were uneventful. Money was not available for exciting building projects. The Priory Stable Block remained half-converted, and the Pilgrims' Hall was still in use as the Dean's chicken house, having been promised by the Chapter to the school once funds could be found for its renovation. The *Magazine*s covering this period tell a tale of continued academic progress and smoothly running routine, with few remarkable events from one year to the next.

The Fifties opened with a spate of illness, which prevented any rugger or hockey matches from being played. The following year, rain had much the same effect. Only one game of hockey was played at all, and in consequence the sport had to be learned anew in 1952. Rugger fared marginally better. The Pilgrims' School was permitted to use the King Alfred's College ground at Bar End, while the inundated Army ground was abandoned to the swans, seagulls and other water-fowl. The flooding also delayed the sowing of the new pitch known as 'Bailey Field'. Although the preparatory levelling and raking had taken place in May 1950, the field was not available for use until the beginning of the Christmas term 1952.

'Lantern lectures' continued, a popular distraction. In 1949 the Winchester Stationmaster and 14 railway employees were invited to a party at the school, after all had attended a lecture by Mr. H. G. Davis on 'British Railways and the Liberation of Europe'. The following year the invitation was extended to no fewer than 19 railwaymen, but the party had to be abandoned owing to the illness of Mr. Davis. Another event which was looked forward to yearly was the visit to the 'assault-at-arms' at the College. This was intended as a reward for those boys who had shown the greatest prowess in gymnastics, and for many years the lucky dozen who attended the display were chosen by Mr. Gear.

The summer of 1950 saw not only the death of Dr. Fogwell, the former Sub-Organist, but also of Mrs. Hoskyns, a benefactress of the school, who had endowed an annual Reading Prize some five years earlier. Thus she missed attending the finals of the 1950 competition, which was judged by Mr. Harry Altham from the College.

In the Easter term of 1951 a student teacher joined the staff: Mr. Rodney Blake. He was so successful that he was invited to join the school as an additional member of staff from the following September. He remained at the school for two years, marrying an assistant matron, Miss Judy Fraser, and left for New Zealand with his new-born son in August 1953.

With the arrival of Rodney Blake, Herbert Smith retired as part-time teacher. As well as teaching the piano and some general academic subjects, Mr. Smith had been the inspiration behind many extra-curricular activities. In preparation for his retirement, he had already handed over the Music Club to the Sub-Organist, Mr. Isidore Harvey. Rodney Blake took charge of the Stamp Club which Mr. Smith had also run.

At the end of 1951, Mr. Winston Churchill and members of His Majesty's Government were to set sail from Southampton on the *Queen Mary*, bound for the United States. Their departure was delayed by a fouled anchor chain. The Dean got to hear of this and quickly arranged an impromptu visit by the Choir, who sang carols to the passengers in the first-class lounge. Unfortunately, Mr. Churchill was 'in conference' but Mr. Anthony Eden made a short speech of thanks, expressing the pleasure and gratitude of the audience.

Meanwhile, new developments were planned. Every year, the number of boys in the school had edged higher, and by 1953 was standing at seventy-six. Space was beginning to run short. At the Pilgrims' School Society meeting of 1952, Donald McLachlan had expressed the hope that 'every effort would be made to improve the finances of the school so that further expansion could take place in the historic buildings connected with it'. The following year, the executive committee of the Society offered 'a contribution of £250 if a Trust will make a grant sufficient to restore the other half of the Priory Stables so as to provide much needed additional accommodation'. By the end of 1955, a grant of £2,500 had been obtained from the Pilgrim Trust and the Historic Buildings Council and the society increased their promised contribution to £500, raising money by the sale of Christmas cards and other means. However, it was a further two years before building work began on the northern section of the Priory Stables.

In November 1954, the Choir participated in two television broadcasts from Winchester Cathedral. The Choristers were quite used to sound broadcasting. The BBC had transmitted Choral Evensong on the Home Service many times since the War, and they had been heard as far away as Venezuela, where Michael Salwey happened to tune in to an Overseas Service repeat transmission, but this was the first time that television cameras had appeared in the Cathedral.

The first programme, broadcast on a Friday night, was a half-hour survey of the architecture and history of the Cathedral, introduced by Basil Taylor. This short programme was of necessity well-rehearsed, for in those early days of television there were no facilities for pre-recording and everything had to be perfect in the live transmission. The Choir appeared briefly in the final sequence. They were heard singing Wood's *Magnificat in E flat*, and gradually the camera moved from the newly-restored roof of the Quire onto the singers themselves.

This programme, like Sunday Mattins two days later, was relayed to France by the ORTF. The arrangements for relaying the service were made at the last minute. It was suddenly realised that French protestants might be interested in viewing an Anglican service, and it must have been the first time an English Cathedral service was seen live in French homes. In its way, it seemed to foreshadow the Cathedral Choir's trip to Paris, nearly 24 years later, when the Choristers sang Evensong in Notre-Dame Cathedral – another 'first'.

Early in the summer of 1955, the total number of scholarships and exhibitions won by Pilgrims' boys reached triple figures. Among those who contributed to the 'century' was Adam Ridley, who had fallen ill with mumps during the Eton Election examination but managed to complete the papers in the Sanatorium at Eton Wick and was placed seventh in the Election.

In July that year, the Queen visited Winchester, just as her parents had done, nine years earlier. She arrived at Wolvesey field, now considerably extended by the addition of 'Bailey', and was cheered by a crowd of over 4,000 schoolchildren. After the traditional *Ad Portas* ceremony at Winchester College, where Her Majesty was welcomed in Latin by the Prefect of Hall, the Queen and the Duke of Edinburgh attended various events in the City, returning to the Cathedral in the late afternoon. They emerged by the South Door, to face a battery of cameras held by the boys of The Pilgrims' School, assembled on the Close Green. Here, the Dean presented Mr. and Mrs. Salwey and the Senior Commoner, Adam Ridley. Her Majesty requested three days to be added to the school holidays.

To commemorate the Queen's visit to Winchester, the City authorities commissioned a portrait of Her Majesty, which now hangs in the Banqueting Hall of the Guildhall. She is depicted apparently seated by the north window of the Priory Stable Block, with the Deanery and Cathedral in the background. In actual fact, the room, which is now known by the inelegant title of P1, was virtually a ruin at the time!

The winter of 1955–6 was saddened by the deaths of a number of men who, in their different ways, had been closely connected with the life of the school. On 8 December R.S.M. Starr died. He had coached shooting at Winchester College since 1919 and instructed the 20 best Pilgrims' School 'shots' since 1938. On 27 January, Spencer Leeson, then Bishop of Peterborough, passed away: the man who had been such an influential member of the school's Advisory Council during the early years. Just one month later, the death of Dr. Harold Rhodes was announced.

It was a cold winter, and, just as they had done during the record low temperatures of February and March 1947, the boys profited from the unusual conditions by learning to skate on the ponds at Winnall. When at last warmer weather came, and it was time to think of summer activities, the City Council decided to close the Bull Drove Baths, which had been used by boys from three Winchester Cathedral schools since the end of the 19th century. Fortunately, the College permitted The Pilgrims' School to use their swimming facilities at 'Gunners Hole' on four mornings a week. Not only were these baths considerably nearer than Garnier Road, but the boys could also benefit from the expert tuition of Mr. Egginton, the College P.T. Instructor.

In July 1956 the school celebrated its Silver Jubilee. The afternoon began with a cricket match between an Old Boy team (captained by Peter Rooke, one of the 'aboriginals') and the First XI. After tea in a marquee in the garden, Old Pilgrims, parents and friends visited an exhibition of handicrafts in the Priory Room. At five o'clock, everyone moved into a large marquee in Mirabel Close to hear the speeches.

The Bishop of Winchester recalled the part he had played in the foundation of the school, as Headmaster of the College in 1931, and called upon Professor Christopher Longuet-Higgins to speak on behalf of the Old Boys. Referring to the 'Sets', Professor Longuet-Higgins noted that there were now four of them, compared with the two of his own schooldays, and he wondered prophetically 'when the Norman invasion was going to begin'. (The Normans Set was formed in September 1966.) Then Sir Eric James, Pilgrims' parent and High Master of Manchester Grammar School, spoke, attributing the success of the school to the Salweys and thanking them on behalf of the parents. Mr. Salwey replied to these speeches, expressing his gratitude for the devotion of his staff, many of whom had served so long, and reviewing the events of the previous 25 years. He also took the opportunity of mentioning the plans for developing the rest of the Priory Stables and the Pilgrims' Hall. Finally, Dean Selwyn summed up the appreciation of all those present for the work done by the Headmaster and Mrs. Salwey. 'It is an extraordinary thing', he commented, 'but I don't think Mr. and Mrs. Salwey look any older than they did when they came here, twenty-five years ago. I think that is probably a great tribute to the boys.'

The Bishop, as Chairman, adjourned the meeting so that those present, more than 500, could attend an Evensong of Thanksgiving in the Cathedral. This started with the Anthem *God be in my Head*, which was always sung at the end of school concerts. The setting of the Evening Canticles was *Stanford in B flat*, and the Anthem was Parry's *I was glad*. The School Prayer was used, which the Dean had composed some years before, and which was invariably said on the last morning of every term.

> Almighty and everliving God, who didst will that men should come as pilgrims to the shrine of St Swithun at Winchester: shed thy blessing, we beseech Thee, on the school that bears their name: knit together the hearts of all its members, whether past or present, in loving loyalty to Thee and to one another. Prosper them in their several callings; and in all time of adversity, be their shield and guide. And grant that in the power of the Holy Spirit, they may be enabled to show forth Thy glory.

At the end of the Christmas term, work began on the north end of the Priory Stabling, which since 1939 had presented a curiously half-finished appearance. While the south end had been renovated, re-tiled and rendered, the northern part, still separated from the Yard by the wall that Humphrey Salwey had attacked on the eve of the War, was in a considerable state of decay. The restoration involved renewing much of the infilling of the east wall at first-floor level, and plastering the walls both inside and out, inserting new windows, building a second large dormer window to light the first-floor classroom and a staircase to provide access to the room at the northern end, and re-tiling the northern section of the stables.

Within a few months it was possible to use one of the new classrooms. Parents, Old Boys and other contributors to the restoration were given an opportunity of viewing the improvements during the Half-Term of June 1957, when an exhibition of mathematical models, devised by Mr. Payton, was held in the Priory Room. One distinguished visitor to the exhibition was the legendary Clem Durell of Winchester College, whose name, in the days before New Maths, was as familiar to schoolboys as the name of Kennedy still is to Latinists.

Appropriately, at the end of the summer term the prizes were presented by Sir Alan Lascelles, Chairman of the Pilgrim Trust and the Historic Buildings Council, which had made such generous contributions towards the cost of restoring the Priory Stables and the Pilgrims' Hall.

In 1955 Dean Selwyn had announced his intention of retiring 'in three years' time'. Thus in 1958 Dean Sykes was installed in his place, but Gordon Selwyn's retirement was cut short by his early death in June the following year. During his 27-year period of office he had created many of the institutions that now seem so essential to the life of the Cathedral: the 'Broderers', the Friends of the Cathedral and, above all, The Pilgrims' School. He had given his backing to many schemes to improve and beautify the church: the restoration of the Presbytery ceiling, the refurbishing of the Cathedral Library's Exhibition Room, the re-hanging of the bells and the rebuilding of the organ.

Well-known in wider circles both as scholar and preacher, he had been equally at home when chatting to the Choristers or reading to the four boys chosen to lodge at the Deanery. He had insisted on preparing boys for Confirmation, in conjunction with Mr. Salwey, and had taken a lively interest in all their affairs. Describing the school which he had created, in his final sermon, preached on St Swithun's Day 1958, he had said:

> The School embodies all I cherish most in education: good teaching and training

in the Christian life, and that combination of discipline with happiness which makes it a Family as well as a School, and illustrates St Paul's saying that 'Love is the fulfilling of the Law'. What can gladden a man's heart more than to see his hopes and ideals come to fruition?

By the spring of 1958, the restoration of the Priory Stable Block was complete: a project that had taken 20 years from beginning to end. The school's new facilities consisted of two large classrooms on the first floor (now the Library and Choristers' Practice Room), two rather smaller rooms below, for handicrafts and the Science Club as well as for teaching, and three music practice rooms. At last it was possible to relinquish the Dome Alley classrooms, although Mr. Steve Blake continued his carpentry classes there until 1963, while the contractors working on the Pilgrims' Hall used the school carpentry room as their workshop. The old playground in Dome Alley became the domain of the Cathedral building staff, and the enlarging of The Pilgrims' School yard was in sight. In 1963 the Dome Alley classrooms were converted into two cottages for the Cathedral staff. Appropriately enough, Mr. Steve Blake (who then retired from his part-time job as carpentry master and was later appointed Clerk of Works) was actively involved in this building scheme, and later moved into one of the cottages he had helped to convert.

In July 1958 a new master joined the staff from the Dragon School, Oxford. Dick Kitson, classical scholar of Rugby and Trinity College, Cambridge, and (as 'Hampshire Hog' and 'Butterfly') cricketer of no mean ability, was a significant acquisition, both in the classroom and on the games field. He immediately took over the running of the Music Club, in succession to the Sub-Organist, Mr. Isidore Harvey, who had retired from his part-time music post at the school.

At the same time, Mr. Rodney Blake, who had returned from New Zealand the previous year, founded a 'Play Reading Society' which, like the Music and Stamp Club, met on Saturday evenings during the winter terms. A timetable had to be devised to cope with these numerous extra-curricular activities. The Play Reading Society gave 'acted readings' of a considerable volume of English drama, and a collection of gramophone recordings of well-known plays was formed. After a few years, the society quietly died, without having ever put on any major production on the Pilgrims' Hall stage, as was hoped. The 'Pilgrims' Players' founded by Neville Ollerenshaw in the early Thirties and revived by Anthony Cussans, had met with a similar fate.

A more successful dramatic venture was the production of *Noyes Fludde* in the Cathedral, performed twice daily for three days in July 1960. Alwyn Surplice was the musical director, conducting a cast of nearly 200 children, including three Choristers, who played the parts of Shem, Ham and Jaffett. According to the *Cathedral Record*, 'the production not only redeemed St Swithun's week from the melancholy rains but attained a new high-water mark in the history of our Cathedral music and drama. Rarely, if ever, has the dais in the Nave presented such a moving and colourful spectacle as that of Noah's family, both human and animal, assembled in the ark as the heavens opened and the floods descended.'

A few months earlier it had been announced that Rodney Blake was to be appointed the school's first Deputy Headmaster in 1961, with a view to taking over the Headmastership on the retirement of Humphrey Salwey; thus the tran-

XXIV The north end of the Priory Stabling before conversion

XXV July 1963. Demolition work in the school yard prior to construction of the 'Salwey Building'. Only one wall of the former stable remains

sition between Headmasters would be achieved smoothly and with minimum disruption to the school. This nomination was one of the last acts of Dean Sykes during his short decanate. He fell ill later that year, and died the following March. He was succeeded in December 1961 by Dean Gibbs-Smith, former Canon Residentiary of St Paul's Cathedral and Archdeacon of London.

At the end of the school year, in July 1962, Dean Gibbs-Smith presented the prizes in the restored Pilgrims' Hall: the first official ceremony to take place in this addition to the school facilities. He paid special tribute to the Salweys, and above all to Lorna Salwey, who was about to retire from her demanding duties of looking after the entire domestic side of the school – no small task in the days before catering managers, domestic bursars and school secretaries. The Dean introduced Andrew Fairbairn, who thanked Mrs. Salwey for all she had done and presented her with a pendant-brooch and a cheque on behalf of the Old Boys.

Thus the transition period began. That September Rodney Blake took up his appointment as Headmaster Designate, living in the school and looking after all domestic arrangements, health and 'House' discipline, while Mr. Salwey, now living at St Cross, retained control of the scholastic staff, the academic side of the school and general discipline.

The total number of boys in the school had now risen to 82, and a new form was created. John Walters had joined the staff, combining the part-time occupation of a Lay Clerk with his full-time duties as a schoolmaster. There were now nine forms, which created problems of accommodation. The Priory Room was used for teaching, as well as the five other classrooms in the stables, and the Library was also called into service.

Further expansion was in sight. Dean Gibbs-Smith was reponsible for moving the Sunday morning services from the Quire of the Cathedral to the Nave. He felt that a larger body of singers was needed and decided to raise the total number of Choristers and Probationers from 20 to 24 boys. In order to finance this expansion, the number of Commoner boarders and dayboys was to be proportionally increased. These plans were outlined in the 1963 *Magazine*.

> The immediate prospect is a total of about 88 boys in September 1963; 90 in January 1964, and ultimately perhaps a total of 99 boys: 74 boarders and 25 day-boys.

A wide-ranging building scheme was announced: the changing room was to be enlarged, and accommodation for three resident masters created above it. A new teaching block was to be built between the changing room and the Priory Stabling, on the site of the double garages, with a new classroom (the present Computer Room) on the first floor and a 'Hobbies and Carpentry Room' (the present Technology and Model Room) downstairs. This room would have to house the Railway as far as possible, for the old attic railway room was to be converted into a dormitory.

Other changes were planned in the Main Building. Extra washing facilities would be required, and a 'Senior Washroom' was planned in the old linen room. The dining hall was to be enlarged by reducing the Junior Classroom by a third of its size, building a blockwork wall between the two and removing the folding doors. To compensate for this, the cloakroom was to be partitioned into 'Toyes' for the senior boys, along Winchester College lines, and the coats, boots and shoes were to be kept in the new changing room.

Finally, the Pilgrims' Hall was to be equipped with a proper heating system. Connected to the Hall near the Library would be a new kitchen and washrooms, to widen the possible uses of the Hall, which was hired out for private functions.

The builders moved in on Monday 10 June 1963, and within a few days almost the whole of the changing room was demolished, together with the common room and garage block.

The disruption caused by building projects in almost every part of the school buildings did not prevent a major dramatic production in the Pilgrims' Hall during the summer of 1963, as part of the Cathedral Close 'Open Day' devised by Dean Gibbs-Smith. The Pilgrims' School's contribution consisted of two performances of an operetta, *The Boy Mozart*, by John Simpson, who had recently joined the music staff. This play, with substantial musical interludes, depicted the arrival of Leopold Mozart after a day's hunting: about 40 boys were involved altogether, and the cast of principals was ingeniously doubled by forming two casts, so that the principals of one performance became 'extras' (sundry Lords and Ladies) in the other.

Demand for seats far exceeded the limited space of the Pilgrims' Hall, which was being used for a dramatic venture for the first time, and parents and friends were encouraged to attend two full dress rehearsals. There were two performances on the 'Open Day', and the operetta brought in nearly £100 towards the Cathedral Close and School Building Improvement funds. The venture was so successful that a year later, just before leaving The Pilgrims' School, John Simpson wrote and produced a similar operetta entitled *Mr. Handel*.

The Christmas term of 1963, Humphrey Salwey's last term as Headmaster, was marked by a frenzy of building activity. Later he described the 'organised chaos' in which he taught: 'the noise, the dirt, the really splendid workmen passing in and out. Often we found ourselves in class shouting down the energies of a monstrous bulldozer just outside the window; or teaching elementary Greek while a carpenter erected lockers on the opposing wall; or correcting books with the floor-boards up while plumbers worked in the depths below.'

At his final prize-giving in the Pilgrims' Hall, when Humphrey Salwey presented the awards himself, Dean Gibbs-Smith announced that the new extension between the changing room and the Priory Stabling was to be known as the 'Salwey Building'. As Harry Altham wrote in a tribute for the *Magazine*:

It must be with a sense of satisfaction that Pilgrims of every generation will read on a plaque the simple words 'The Salwey Building'. For surely the school as we know it today stands indebted for all time to two men: to Dean Selwyn for the vision and initiative that launched it, and to Humphrey Salwey for the dedication with which for 32 years he gave himself to making of it what he felt a school should be.

He will be remembered first and foremost as a man who knew where he was going and where he wanted others to go: a man of principles on which he would never compromise, and of standards which, whether for himself or others, staff or boys, he would never relax.

A sound scholar, he believed wholeheartedly in the Classics as a basic discipline for the mind, and an inescapable challenge from which carelessness or even the 'nearly right' must never be allowed to escape; and it was his teaching that year by year laid the foundations for that astonishing record of 125 Scholarships or Exhibitions.

On 28 December 1963 about 90 Old Pilgrims gathered at the Cadena in Winchester for a dinner, at which a cheque was presented to Humphrey and Lorna Salwey, intended to enable them to visit their family in New Zealand. In his farewell speech, the retiring Headmaster explained how he had accidentally discovered the true nature of the 'small dinner party' to which he had been invited.

> For better or worse, I had just been re-elected Chairman of the City Bench for the sixth year, and as such was hearing applications for occasional licences, when a local solicitor rose and said, 'I find it very difficult to make my application as long as you are on the Bench'. Wondering whether or not to take umbrage, I looked hard at him, and enquired if he was really aiming at me, whereupon he said, 'I am making application for a large number of Old Boys to entertain someone whom we all know well'. That gave me my first clue!

Reviewing the events of the previous 32 years, Humphrey Salwey paid tribute to the various people who had assisted him: Mrs. Salwey, 'my constant advisor and companion', the teaching and domestic staff, the Governing Body and the Advisory Council.

'And so', he concluded, 'Chapter I is ended: Chapter II immediately begins. We both wish to Rodney and Judy Blake all possible good health, success, and the same happiness that we have had. I know that under him and all who will serve with him, the school will reach to greater heights as the years go by. To the school then as a family, I would just say *"Floreat"*.'

Chapter Eight

YEARS OF EXPANSION

AT HUMPHREY SALWEY'S RETIREMENT a number of changes occurred on the teaching staff. Miss Cunningham left, after 13 years as part-time Scripture mistress, and was replaced by Jane Stear. Miss Harvey retired after 21 years as junior form teacher, and Miss Butler's long association with the music both of The Pilgrims' School and its two predecessors also came to an end.

In January 1964 Mr. Ferguson was appointed part-time Science master, to take the top three forms for two lessons per week. He had run the Science Club since 1947, and although this society continued its activities for a further year or two, it was clear that the new Headmaster wished to see Science elevated to the status of a timetabled subject. Indeed, Rodney Blake had for the previous two years been teaching some elementary Science to the senior boys, using the 'science kits' which arrived weekly, courtesy of Esso Petroleum.

That summer, Mr. Ferguson gained further experience of teaching Science to young beginners when he attended a special course at Loughborough. These were the early days of 'Nuffield Science', and The Pilgrims' School was invited to take part in the pilot scheme for working out the new approach: the 'Nuffield Biology Project'.

The Science Club rapidly came to an end. In its hey-day, it had provided a valuable introduction to elementary physics and chemistry for a limited number of boys (22 or so at the most), and the synopsis of activities, listed every year in the *Magazine*, bore witness to Mr. Ferguson's thoroughness. With the growth of the Science Department, covering similar topics, the club became redundant.

In June 1964, a year to the day after their noisy arrival, the builders left. Their efforts had provided considerable space for the expanding school population, including the extra classroom on the first floor of the Salwey Extension which at first was used as a classroom for the most junior form, and later as the Science Room.

Further space for less formal activities was provided during that summer term when the Dean made a stretch of his garden available to the school as a play area. This concession provided considerable scope for the adventurous. 'After Half-Term', noted the editor of the *Magazine*, 'a variety of "Dean's Garden Clothes" was brought back to school; and on half-holidays and Sundays an assortment of coloured shirts and sweaters was to be seen disappearing over the wall into this new territory: some quickly pitching their tents, while others, finding a suitable supply of corrugated iron, had soon built their own houses; and even a floating pier was seen on the river.'

Rodney Blake began his first complete school year as Headmaster by introducing a complex system of 'Gilds' in an attempt to breathe new life into 'Handicrafts' and to provide a competitive element in the exercise of manual skills. 'There are four Gilds', he explained in the *Magazine*, 'labelled Art, Arts, Science and Craft; and within each Gild there are four different levels. Each boy begins as a Novice, and by taking certain tests, works his way up through Apprentice, Journeyman and Master levels. Once a boy has achieved the status of a Journeyman in two Gilds, having already become an Apprentice in four, he is awarded his tie for Gild work.'

Innovations were not restricted to out-of-school activities. At about the same time, the teaching of Modern Languages was rejuvenated, by adopting the CREDIF Audio-Visual French course with the most junior boys. This proved most effective, and a valuable introduction to the more formal methods of the ever-conscientious Mr. Gardner.

Television cameras frequently appeared in the Cathedral during the early Sixties. During the Christmas term of 1964, John Betjeman had introduced a programme from the Cathedral on BBC Television, and in March 1965 Southern Television began its long association with the Cathedral, filming a short feature for *Day by Day*, illustrating a day in the life of a Chorister. The Head Chorister, Mark Graveson, was filmed practising in the Pilgrims' Hall with the rest of the Choristers, in a Latin lesson, and, finally, singing in the Cathedral. A little more than a year later the BBC produced a radio programme, *The Choristers*, with much the same theme, a 45-minute broadcast on the Home Service. All 20 Choristers and several members of staff were interviewed, and the programme included a 'Voice Trial', in which a Chorister, Robin Clitherow, played the part of the aspiring applicant. This programme was felt to be more successful than the BBC's attempt at a televised *Life of a Chorister* three years earlier.

That spring, work began on a school tennis court, at the expense of part of the elegant garden of No.3 The Close. Mr. Fitzmaurice, who had returned to the school on a part-time basis after a successful hip operation the previous term, was the inspiration behind this project. He provided a generous contribution himself, the Pilgrims' School Society donated £300, and the Dean and Chapter met the balance of the costs. Appropriately, 'Fitz' opened the tennis court himself, at the end of May 1965, and scored the first point on the court, in a short game against the Headmaster.

Meanwhile, rehearsals went ahead for a major dramatic production, *A Midsummer Night's Dream*, produced by John Walters. This was to have taken place during the Easter term, but the cast fell variously victim to mumps, measles and chicken-pox, and the play had to be postponed until the end of June. Despite all these difficulties, the production was voted a resounding success. It was appreciated rather more than John Walters' esoteric venture of the following year, a performance of *Samson Agonistes*.

At the end of the academic year, Rodney Blake ensured that parents had ample opportunity of witnessing the achievements of their sons in various fields. Two young musicians devised a concert in which much of the music was written by themselves. Not to be outdone, the less musical contributed items to the exhibition of project work in the Priory Room, or took part in recitations, French playlets or Latin verse readings.

Newcomers to the staff in September 1965 included Frank Skipwith, and an Old Pilgrim, James Larcombe, who joined the newly formed Science Department. At the end of the previous term, Mr. Ferguson had been highly commended by the co-ordinators of the Nuffield Biology Project, and it was felt that the boys should now have the opportunity of studying some physics.

Those parents who had visited the school at the end of the previous term were apparently impressed. There was as yet no 'Parents' Association', but a number of enthusiastic mothers and fathers formed a Swimming Pool Committee to raise funds for a 'Pilgrims' Pool' next to the tennis court. Money was raised in a variety of ways: by direct appeal, by tombola and raffles, and by an elegant dinner-dance held at Avington Park. The Pilgrims' School Society donated £500. Thus work was able to start by the end of April 1966, and the pool was ready for use by 10 June, an impressive achievement on the part of the contractors. The new pool was intended mainly for recreational purposes and for the instruction of non-swimmers, while for more serious competitive swimming and diving the Gunners Hole facilities continued to be used until the College Sports Centre opened in February 1969.

That same summer Dean Gibbs-Smith allowed the school to take over a further portion of his garden for use as cricket nets, and the old hard nets at Blackbridge Yard were abandoned.

At about the same time the school was allowed the use of a sizeable field in College Walk, 'New Piece'. This land, together with three classrooms at No.12 College Street, were the dowry brought by 15 Quiristers from Winchester College, who joined the school on an experimental basis in September 1966.

The historically aware may have called to mind the similar experiments of the 19th century which had never lasted more than a few months, it seems, but the new merger was more carefully planned. The previous October, details had appeared in the newspapers of the two-year trial period during which the Quirister School of Winchester College would be associated for educational purposes with The Pilgrims' School. 'Quiristers will continue to receive their musical education at the College', the notice continued, 'but for their work and play they will join The Pilgrims' School.'

Earlier in the summer of 1966, Quirister parents had been invited to meet members of The Pilgrims' staff at a sherry party. They were taken on a tour of the school premises, and attended the last of three performances of the operetta *The Bride of Seville*, performed by the Quiristers in the Pilgrims' Hall.

Before the merger, the education of the Quiristers at their house in Kingsgate Street had been undertaken by one man, John Weekes, Housemaster since 1936. He was, however, helped by members of the College staff, including the Headmaster and the Chaplains, who would come across to take the Quiristers in Mathematics, Divinity and certain other subjects. The Quiristers used the College facilities for Art, Handicrafts, P.T. and, for a time, Science.

'Singing and instrumental music of course took place in Music School under the music staff', recalls John Weekes. 'Some of the brighter boys were allowed to do Maths or French in the "Junior Part" set of the College: a few would join the College Divisions for all subjects, while continuing to be Quiristers in other ways. Coaching was given in cricket, football and swimming.'

In September 1966 John Weekes joined the Pilgrims' staff for a short time before retiring, and John and Claire Walters moved to Quiristers' School, taking with them 14 Commoner boarders. Meanwhile five Quiristers slept in the senior dormitories at 'Main School', and in this way, the new boys – still wearing their distinctive blue uniform – were integrated into the life of the school as fully and as rapidly as possibly.

In the expectation of the experiment proving successful, the Dean and Chapter had optimistically made provision for the incorporation of the Quiristers' School in the revised Cathedral Statutes of 1967.

... In the event of the permanent incorporation of the Quirister School of Winchester College with the Pilgrims' School, the Dean & Chapter shall invite the Warden & Fellows of Winchester College to nominate two additional persons to the Governing Body.

The merger was finally sealed in 1978, when the Headmaster of the College and one other representative became members of the Governing Body.

The inclusion of the Quiristers was only a contributory factor to a dramatic population explosion during the years 1965-7. There were 85 boys in the school in 1965, 104 the following year, and an astonishing 150 in 1967!

Many of the newcomers were dayboys. As we have seen, their numbers were modest in the early years of the school, restricted almost entirely to the sons of Winchester College dons, clergy, and parents with an existing involvement with the school. During the Headmastership of Humphrey Salwey, 18 was the average number of dayboys, though the proportion increased somewhat during the Fifties. However, between 1966 and 1967, the number of dayboys doubled, from 30 to 60! A 'Master in Charge of Dayboys' was appointed, and a new Set was created, the 'Normans', thus fulfilling Professor Longuet-Higgins' prediction of 11 years before.

The increase in numbers presented considerable problems of organisation. It was no longer possible for the entire school to eat together in the dining hall, and despite the acquisition of 'New Piece' (and the use of 'Palmer Field', granted a year later), the school's games facilities were inadequate. There were, fortunately, just enough classrooms, and to facilitate movement to and from the newly acquired classrooms next door to Wells' bookshop, the Dean and Chapter allowed the old passageway between the Yard and College Street to be opened up again.

In order to cope with the increased numbers, the school was divided into senior and junior halves, with five forms in each. Lunches were taken in two sittings, so that the juniors could eat early and complete their games before the seniors arrived at the pitches. By keeping groups of boys moving around the school premises, it was possible to create an illusion of adequate space.

If the expansion of 1966 was unsettling for the boys – 'more than a little confusing', as the *Magazine* described the beginning of the new school year – it was hardly less turbulent for the teaching and domestic staff. Until this time, the

Common Room appears remarkably permanent in composition, with an impressive record of long service given by a small number of men and women, some of whom devoted virtually the whole of their career to the school. Changes of personnel were infrequent and have been recorded during the course of this narrative. Between 1965 and 1968, however, more than 20 people joined or left the staff. It is true that several of these changes involved temporary masters, often Old Pilgrims filling in the gap between school and university. Nevertheless, the overall effect seems to have been to unsettle still further a school already struggling in its efforts to accommodate 150 boys in premises designed for 60.

The expansion of the school thus created great pressures upon the teaching staff, and not least upon the Headmaster. Gone was the family atmosphere of earlier decades, Spencer Leeson's idea that 'We should not be a large school: we should be a large family'. Almost overnight, Pilgrims' had expanded into a school of considerable size, with all the administrative problems that such an institution creates. Even the appointment of a permanent bursarial and secretarial staff failed to relieve the pressure.

In September 1967 the school's form structure was completely re-organised with the creation of the present 'Block' system and, for the more senior boys, 'setting' in four major subjects: 'Maths, & Science', 'English Subjects', French, and Latin. Three junior forms were created for the lower third of the school: JJ (the Junior form), JM (after the form-mistress, Marjory Monro) and JT (after Mr. Tewkesbury). The purpose of this re-organisation was to ensure that both the future scholars and boys of more modest scholastic ability were taught to the limits of their potential. An inevitable consequence of the enlarging of the school and ensuing broadening of the intake was an increasing proportion of the less academically-inclined, and for several years the proportion of leavers to obtain scholarships was significantly lower than it had been in the past. Such was the short-term consequence of expansion, and it would be some time before the benefits of the restructuring of the forms was felt.

Another sad result of the rapid growth of the school was the gradual erosion of spare time and the closure of many of the clubs and societies that had flourished in earlier days, when the staff were less over-worked and the timetable less dominated by the need to keep the pupils moving around in order to share the inadequate dining and games facilities.

The Railway Club suffered least. The old track was re-laid in the Priory Stable Block, but the old Bassett-Lowke system was soon to be sold, at a fraction of its present value, in order to purchase a double-O gauge lay-out. The new electric railway proved extremely popular for a time, and in 1968 the club attracted as many as 68 members. There was a further burst of enthusiasm more recently when the track was re-laid among carefully-landscaped cliffs and mountains, and the club has a popular following.

The Stamp Society closed after a year or two. Other clubs were institutionalised, like the Science Club (which lost its appeal once Science had assumed a place on the timetable) and the Wildlife Club, which survives in annual lectures by the Director of the World Wildlife Youth Service, visits to the R.S.P.B. 'Bird Films' at the Guildhall and, especially, Mary Taylor's 'Naturewatch' club. A short-lived Angling Club – apparently diametrically opposed in its aims to the conservation-minded Wildlifers – organised infrequent visits to likely locations, but its members returned empty-handed each time!

Ironically the Music Club was disbanded (except for occasional visits to concerts) shortly after the appointment of The Pilgrims' School's first director of music, Miss Sybil Norgarb. Music undoubtedly benefited from the expansion of the school, in that a greater pool of talent was available, notably the Quiristers, some of whom already played in the College Second Orchestra. Shortly after her arrival, Miss Norgarb formed a Pilgrims' School Orchestra. During its early days this included some rather unorthodox instruments – guitars, recorders and the like – and performances relied heavily on piano stiffening. It would be some years before performances reached the standards to which we are now accustomed. Although there had been some outstanding individual instrumentalists, the general standard of playing was not high, if the number and level of Associated Board passes is a guide. One particular problem, noted by Her Majesty's Inspectors during their visit of 1970, was a lack of facilities: three practice rooms had been barely adequate for a school of 70 and the school was now twice as large.

The greater available forces meant also that school dramatic productions could become more ambitious. *Samson Agonistes* was followed in 1967 by Obey's *Noah*, which proved more to the boys' taste, and in which Frank Skipwith demonstrated his skill as a designer of stage sets. Meanwhile, the Quiristers continued their independent operatic productions with performances of *Bastien et Bastienne* by Mozart, and Kurt Weill's *Der Jasager*, produced by Grahame Drew of Winchester College. However, the major dramatic event of the Sixties was perhaps the *Bakelite Affair*, reviewed in style in the *Magazine* of 1968.

> If you can imagine a mystery musical dressed in Monks' Habit, add two village maidens named Beaujolais and Marsala, a landlord called Hamburger and a baddy Bart, who is also an A.R.C.M., you are getting close to the *Bakelite Affair*, written and produced by Clement McWilliam and staged at the end of the spring term in the Pilgrims' Hall by a combination of Choristers, Commoners, hard work and enthusiasm.

Perhaps the Choristers were, in their official activities at least, less affected by the expansion of The Pilgrims' School than any other group of boys. The round of daily services, choir-times and the Southern Cathedrals Festival continued unhindered and unchanged. The Choir could now count on the support of the Winchester Cathedral Old Choristers' Association, which had been disbanded in 1931 when the Choir School was closed and which was re-formed some 30 years later, with ex-Chorister Jimmy Burchell as Secretary and Eric Greene as Chairman. Alwyn Surplice did much to further Mr. Burchell's hopes that Old Choristers could return and be made welcome at Winchester at any time.

The Southern Cathedrals Festival had been revived in 1960 by Dr. Surplice and his fellow-organists at Chichester and Salisbury, and provided exciting opportunities for the choirs of the three cathedrals to perform music needing unusually large forces, like the *Chichester Psalms* of Leonard Bernstein, first performed in Chichester Cathedral during the 1965 S.C.F., in the presence of the composer. Avant-garde music, tempered by more traditional compositions, remains a feature of today's Southern Cathedrals Festival programmes.

Until 1966, Christmas choir-time had always continued until the end of December. With the incorporation of the Quiristers, the Pilgrims' School terms had to start rather earlier, in line with Winchester College, and Dean Gibbs-Smith, an ex-chorister of King's College Cambridge, evidently felt that the Cathedral was demanding too great a sacrifice of the Choristers' family life. Thus, from that Christmas, the boys were allowed to go home after Evensong on Christmas Day.

In October 1966 the Choristers had taken part in an overseas trip, the first since 1949. This was to mark the anniversary of a fellow Benedictine foundation, the Abbey Church of Mont-Saint-Michel in Brittany. The Choir participated in a Roman Catholic Mass and an Anglican Evensong. In stark contrast to the earlier trips to the Channel Islands, the weather remained resolutely wet and windy, and the Choristers returned from foreign parts as impressed by the foulness of the climate as by the success of the music which they had sung.

The Choristers no longer held the monopoly of singing in The Pilgrims' School. Apart from the Quiristers, an active Commoners' Choir had begun to make its presence felt. It performed a number of carols at the school's first Carol Service in the Cathedral, in 1966, and the following year visited Hampton Court to sing Evensong in the Chapel there.

Gradually, as the Sixties drew to a close, staff and boys learned to cope with the difficulties of overcrowding. School life settled into a routine of a kind. If the boys' activities were of necessity more strictly regimented by the demands of the time-table than they had been in earlier, less crowded days, there were exciting compensations like the summer Expeditions, when the whole school set off in bus-loads to descend on factories, dock-yards and army camps. There was even a cross-Channel trip to see the Bayeux Tapestry, arranged by Mr. Gardner for a lucky group of francophiles, who caught the Channel ferry one blustery October day.

Just as the turbulent effects of the expansion of the school were beginning to diminish, there was a new shock. In the Easter term of 1969 Rodney Blake had been granted a term's leave of absence. A few weeks later he resigned his headmastership for personal reasons.

Meanwhile, Dean Gibbs-Smith, who had suffered from ill-health for a number of years, announced his forthcoming retirement. He died later that summer. Thus much of the business of selecting candidates for the new headmastership fell upon the Vice-Dean, Canon Maundrell, who was himself to resign before the new Headmaster took up his appointment. The final choice of Martin Briggs was made in October 1969 by the Dean-elect, Canon Michael Stancliffe.

Dick Kitson, acting Headmaster during the long interregnum, summed up these changes in the 1970 *Magazine*:

A new Headmaster, a new Dean, several new members of staff: all these make one realise that the school is moving into a new era. Much is written these days of people and institutions being dragged screaming into the Seventies. We hope to achieve the step forward here, certainly, without the screaming; but also without too much need of being dragged: yet we are well aware of the number and size of the challenges that lie ahead.

Chapter Nine

QUIETLY INTO THE SEVENTIES

MARTIN BRIGGS, his wife Margie and their two children moved into the Headmaster's flat on 1 April 1970, thereby involuntarily adding to the school's accommodation problems; for part of their flat had served as a dormitory and French Room during the interregnum, and the school had now expanded by a further 14 boys.

Even before the new Headmaster took up his appointment there had been a number of changes on the staff: notably the retirement of Mr. Payton, who handed over the Maths Department to David Cheetham while continuing to teach form 'C1 Maths' on a part-time basis. Miss Sybil Norgarb had been replaced by Clement McWilliam, Old Pilgrim and no stranger to the Close, having been Alwyn Surplice's sub-organist for two years. John and Claire Walters had moved to Cranbrook School, Kent, and Denis Blake had become the Housemaster of Quiristers' School. Chris Hazelgrove's place as a junior form teacher was taken over for one term by Margaret Morris, who eventually joined the staff in a full-time capacity. Last but not least, Ruth Pruen, later described as a 'matron in a million', arrived just in time to work in close liaison with Margie Briggs in supervising the boys' welfare, and much more.

Towards the end of Martin Briggs' first term, a 'Medieval Pageant and Fair' were arranged, in an effort to raise money for much-needed new classroom facilities. The Pageant, in four short scenes, illustrated the life of Winchester Choristers in Saxon, Medieval, Tudor and Stuart times, ending with the arrival of Oliver Cromwell. The Priory Stabling provided an appropriate background to the drama. Next, an impressive mounted procession made its way down College Street to Wolvesey, where about 20 stalls had been set up. At the end of the afternoon, a Knight in Armour successfully slew a Dragon which appeared from Wolvesey Castle, thus winning the hand of his Lady. There was an amusing sequel, recounted in the *Magazine*:

> Later that evening, when all the boys had returned to bed, the corpse of the Dragon was seen departing from the Close strapped to the roof of a parent's car, presumably to the consternation and alarm of those who spotted it speeding along the main roads of the New Forest on its way back to Poole.

These efforts raised some £344 towards improvements and musical instruments, but it would be some years before the new classroom block called the 'Selwyn Building' was constructed. However, the lack of classroom space was somewhat relieved at the end of 1970, when the College allowed The Pilgrims' School the use of two complete floors in their property known as 'Wellington House', in place of the three rooms at No.12 College Street, which they required for their own purposes. In anticipation of this move, the first-floor classroom at the north end of the Priory Stable Block had been rearranged as a practice room for the Choristers.

There were two celebrations in 1971: the millennary of the Translation of St Swithun, and the 40th anniversary of The Pilgrims' School. During the summer term, Frank Skipwith transformed a farm cart into the semblance of an Ark, and in July a performance of *Noah's Flood* from the Chester Mystery Cycle was given in the school Yard: this was The Pilgrims' School's contribution to the Cathedral Close 'At Home' afternoon. 'The whole cast', wrote a reviewer, 'had worked hard in rehearsal for the one performance, and they had their reward: blazing sunshine, between two and three hundred people, and not one hitch. The mast and sail that had caused so much trouble behaved perfectly, and (thanks to Mr. Skipwith sheltering in the shadow of the Ark, and Mr. Hayward in the Science Laboratory with his fishing-rod) both the Raven and the Dove travelled along the wire with grace and precision.'

Dean Stancliffe, whose association with the school had begun in December 1969 when he presented the prizes at the end of term, preached the sermon at the 40th anniversary service. He alluded to the name given to the school by Humphrey Salwey and Dean Selwyn, and to the School Prayer, and took as his theme the idea of the pilgrimage through life, quoting in its entirety Cavafy's poem *Ithaca*. He concluded

> A Pilgrim is one who journeys in order to reach something high and holy. To arrive there is his ultimate goal. But he does not hurry the journey at all: he prays that the road is long; he buys pleasurable perfumes of all kinds; he learns and learns from those who have knowledge; and he keeps his eyes open and about him, noticing with care a lily in the field on one side and a wounded man in the gutter on the other. It is the journey, not the arrival, that matters – for it is the journey that makes possible the arrival at the heights of holiness.
>
> It is indeed for this cause that this School was founded, and has existed for 40 years to stand, as its name indicates, for these great truths. God grant it will long continue to do so.

At the end of the school's 40th year, Mr. Gardner retired. A note in the *Magazine* reads: 'He joined the staff in September 1936 when the school was a mere five years old. Apart from war service with the RAF he has been here ever since. He has taught English and French with meticulous care, run the Library, patiently coached the shooting, introduced rugger and coached it for several years, has made terrible puns in three or more languages, and has been a fiercely patriotic Set Master of the Monks.'

'He has always been so much a part of the school', wrote one Old Boy, 'that one can somehow never imagine him not being there. He will be remembered for his kindness and his teaching, for such things as shepherding us on the school train, the black tie he always wore on Mondays when the Monks were on duty, his daily wrangle with the crossword puzzle.'

H.M.G. retired to Dorset. Grateful Old Pilgrims contributed towards a generous cheque in thanks for his devoted service.

A few months later, Alwyn Surplice retired. He had held the post of Organist and Master of the Music at Winchester Cathedral for nearly a quarter of a century under four different Deans. He died in 1977, and an appeal was immediately launched to endow a Choristership in the Choir that he had worked so unstintingly to create. Dean Stancliffe's *Appreciation* underlines his unforgettable personal qualities, his kindness, his sensitive and deeply spiritual musical direction.

His work may not have seemed particularly spectacular at the time, but it was he who hopefully, doggedly and very patiently laid the foundations of the Cathedral's music as it is today. In the hard years which followed all the dislocation and stand-still of the Second World War, there was much to be done and little to do it with, and the Cathedral's music was not given a high priority. The unendingly insatiable and costly demands of the building itself came first, and Alwyn had to manage with an inadequately sized choir, a music library badly in need of renewal and no full-time assistant. The frustrations and delays experienced in his first 10 or 12 years might well have disheartened a less courageous man, but Alwyn's initiative in reviving the Southern Cathedrals Festival in 1960 is only one sign that his devotion to the cause of Cathedral music was still burning brightly and steadily. With the coming of Dean Gibbs-Smith, his patience was rewarded and at last it was possible to provide him with more adequate resources and so enable him to create the choir which so great a building deserves.

Alwyn Surplice's successor, Martin Neary, arrived from St Margaret's Church, Westminster, at the beginning of 1972, to build energetically on the foundations laid by his predecessor. One of his first actions was to re-organise the Choristers' routine, putting back the start of Evensong so that men and boys could practise the evening's music before the service. In compensation, the Choristers were given a free evening on Mondays.

While the standard of choral music in the Cathedral continued to rise under the new direction, hardly less noticeable was the improvement in the musical ability of the Commoners. The new Headmaster was an enthusiastic and informed music lover, and he had on his staff a number of talented musicians: John Smith, oboe player; David Cheetham, Patrick Jordan and Richard White, three Cathedral Lay Clerks who, together with Choir colleague and Pilgrims' parent Donald Sweeney, had formed a close-harmony quartet called 'Euphony'; and, for a time, Rory Boyle, composer, pupil of Lennox Berkeley and winner of the Royal Philharmonic Society's prize for a symphony. All five taught some music and David Cheetham ran the Commoners' Choir.

Unfortunately, the facilities for musicians did not match the impressive personnel. Clement McWilliam had underlined the problems in an article written at the end of his first year as Director of Music:

The aim for the distant future is to provide, if at all possible, the very large amount of accommodation required, and this is being considered in the appropriate quarters. In the meanwhile teachers and pupils must cultivate a sense of vision about the possibilities – remembering that The Pilgrims' can and must be one of the outstanding musical schools of its type in the country, not being content with the low standards and mediocre achievement too often found at present.

Some idea of the rise in instrumental ability may be obtained by studying the programmes of school concerts during the Seventies. In the early years of the decade, short solo items were the order of the day: the Orchestra was little more than a 'Band', with a limited and elementary repertoire of watered-down popular classics. For example, in 1972 the orchestra tackled Handel's *March from Scipio*; eight years later, we find the second orchestra tackling the same piece, while the first orchestra has graduated to complex compositions by the Director of Music himself. Chamber music becomes increasingly prevalent, replacing the predictable combinations of solo instrument plus keyboard of earlier years.

Equally significant, and attributable largely to the enthusiasm and talent of Martin Briggs (who among other posts held that of Chairman of the I.A.P.S. English 'Review Committee'), were the dramatic productions of the early Seventies. In 1971 Clement McWilliam wrote, and Ken Tewkesbury produced, a hilarious farce, *The King's Strings*. No less successful was the accompanying 'Staff Entertainment', a staging of Shaw's *Passion, Poison and Petrifaction*. Then there was *Noah's Flood* in the Yard; *Joseph and the Amazing Technicolour Dreamcoat* in 1973 and two acts from Sheridan's *The Critic*, directed by the Headmaster; a second production of McWilliam's *Bakelite Affair* at the end of that year; and the four 'Block Plays' of 1974. At last, the stage of the Pilgrims' Hall was being used to the full. Somehow, time was found for rehearsals.

Other changes were taking place on the games field. Ambrose Streatfeild continued the good work of Dick Kitson and led the First XI to new success; but a rival to cricket had appeared – athletics, now elevated to the rank of a major sport under the leadership of Patrick Jordan. It was he who introduced the Amateur Athletic Association's 'five-star' scheme to the school, whereby boys are encouraged to attempt a wide range of events, thereby gaining points both for their Set and towards a personal certificate and badge. During the first year of the scheme, almost every boy in the school gained at least a one-star award; several amassed enough points in various events to qualify for the coveted five-star badge.

Whereas in earlier years, athletics (in the form of 'The Sports') had been a purely internal affair, 1971 saw the first matches against other schools. The record times and distances show a steady improvement throughout the Seventies, thanks to the careful coaching of Patrick Jordan and his stentorian successor, Colin Thompson.

Nor were the athletic achievements of boys and staff now confined to term-time. Already during the Christmas holidays of 1968, a party of 28 boys had been taken to the Tyrol for the first skiing trip. In spite of a broken ankle and transport troubles involving flight delays, the venture was voted a success, and was repeated under the leadership of Frank Skipwith yearly, beginning in the Easter holidays of 1970. No less successful were the I.A.P.S. Mediterranean Cruises arranged from 1973 by Ambrose Streatfeild, who ran into difficulties in Venice when confronted by an inquisitive Italian tie-seller:

'*Sono tutti vostri figli, questi fanciulli?*'
'*Io sono professore, non padre.*'

Nearer home, three adult Pilgrims and one College Don, Tony Ayres, took part in a formidable perambulation: a walk along the Pilgrims' Way, from Winchester to Canterbury. David Cheetham, Candy Audsley (assistant matron) and the Headmaster's indefatigable secretary Celia Thomas were the other members of the party. The latter two were shortly to leave the school: Miss Audsley for Kenya and Celia Thomas for the Cathedral School in Oxford.

Shortly after their return, Ambrose Streatfeild organised a working party of Choristers to mend the goal-mouths of the Wolvesey soccer pitches, and during the ensuing refreshments in the *Wykeham Arms* composed the following Chaucerian parody:

> There was a Clerk who, when he chose to sing
> As Chanticleer, could make the welkin ring.
> But such his divers art and range of note
> That, when he wished, he sang like Pertelote.
> At Mathematick and at Chemistry
> He was well versed, and eke a Dominee.
> He schooled nat Choristers but Common boys
> To send God up to Heav'n with merry noise
> So artfully that once a term their tune
> Did please both Dean and Congregacioun.
>
> Next cometh Catherine (Candy now y-clept),
> Apprenticed to a Matron, most adept
> And versed in Pruens and other purgatifs,
> In pokkes and scabbes, and boys' malingering sniffs.
> A sweet by name and sweeter of visage
> And nature, who had lately come of age,
> From King's Worthy she came to join Miss Treen,
> A Worthy maid, I trow, to be a Queen.
> Now she has gone to Afric's sunny clime
> To pass a year in temperature sublime.
> 'Blow the wind southerly right soon' we pray,
> 'And waft her back to Winton sans delay'.
>
> A Don hight Ayres, at young Will Wykeham's school
> (Despite which handicap he was no fool),
> A wight of wondrous versatilitie,
> He cooked fine dishes, maked melodye;
> And more – for he had writ a learned boke
> On Physicks – and oft times donned a cloke

To play a merry role upon the stage.
For vertu, he was wont with great courage
To climben mountains, lithe as any catte.
He railed 'This Pilgrims' Way is far too flatte:
It will not put us to the test enow!' –
'Tis Ayres, nat Manners, makyth Man, I trow!

Last, but nat least of such a worthy band
Was Celia, scrivenour in shorte hand.
Oft was it spoke *'In principio*
Mulier est hominis confusio'.
But of fair Celia, truer far, I wis
'Woman is Mannes joy and all his blis'.
A melange of wit and great solempnitee
She drave a yellow car (sans M.O.T.).
With sweete voice wonter to sing soft tunes
She answered sundry wights on telephoons,
And ran nat once but many times a week
The holy blissful Martin for to seek.
Both she and Dickon underwent much stress,
Y-coopèd in their study – natheless
Through six long years she strove to keep her cool
(Digne to be Patron Saint of Pilgrims' School).
She goes with Pilgrims' benisons and grace
To work in Christës Church, a blessed place –
Thrice blessed, such a scrivenour to win:
Certes, she was of Blissful Martyr's kin.
Of her parting, thus singeth everich wight:
"'Tis Winton's woe, but Oxenford's delight".

Perhaps Martin Briggs' most significant contributions to the development of the school during his short headmastership were firstly to face up squarely to the problems of overcrowding that he had inherited, and secondly to involve parents more closely in the running and general activities of the school: vitally important in a preparatory school with an increasing proportion of dayboys.

These two achievements reflected his clear idea of the school's pastoral obligations, and were combined in the Appeal of 1972, which thus had more far-reaching implications than merely raising a large sum of money. A few months after the Appeal had been launched, the Headmaster summarised its primary aims in the *Magazine*:

What we are trying to do, with no increase in numbers, is to improve our classroom accommodation by the provision of more specialist subject rooms and virtually to double the number of rooms available for the teaching of music.

A specialist firm, Richard Maurice Ltd., was called in, and Old Pilgrims, parents and friends were persuaded to contribute a total of no less than £30,000 in the form of covenants: an impressive response. Meanwhile, nearly £3,500 in cash was raised by more spectacular means, like the sponsored swim organised by Frank Skipwith in May 1972, involving every boy in the school, every parent and a great number of friends. The College Pool had been booked for three hours, and over £2,000 was earned through sponsorship during that short time. The Pilgrims' School Society, assisted by the newly formed 'Parents' Committee', organised several fund-raising events: a Harvest Festival Ball brought in over £500, and a similar sum was realised at a bazaar at Half-Term, in November 1972.

A significant side-effect of the Appeal was that it finally proved that The Pilgrims' School could manage its own financial affairs without having to go cap-in-hand to the Chapter whenever any development was planned. It set the seal on an increasingly business-like attitude to the school's finances, initiated by Dean Gibbs-Smith and executed by 'Bunny' Stear, the school's first Bursar, and Canon Bussby, then Cathedral Treasurer. An early triumph came when The Pilgrims' School was allowed its own bank account. Later, the addition to the Governing Body of Winchester College Headmaster John Thorn, and Estates Bursar David Vellacott, lent extra weight to the idea that The Pilgrims' School must be run as an independent and viable business concern, a kind of subsidiary company of the Dean and Chapter. This in turn led to a relationship between the School and the Chapter that was the stronger for the new mutual respect resulting from financial independence.

The new facilities were to consist of a purpose-built classroom block. There being no more ancient buildings to convert, and no further corners of the 'yard' to develop, the only available site was in the garden, where a cedar tree had stood for many years. Planning permission was granted in August 1973, tenders were invited for the construction work, and a few weeks later the cedar tree was felled – the first operation in the new development.

It was some months before building began. The contractors arrived early in April 1974 and excavated foundation trenches. Those who hoped for exciting archaeological discoveries like those made in 1933 were disappointed: it seemed that this part of Winchester had not been built on before, and the only 'find' was a fragment of a Bellarmine ware bottle. The foundation trenches had to be dug deep in the soft alluvial deposits, down to at least 15 feet, and the excavations quickly filled with water, being well below the water table at that time of year.

The Close gates were too narrow for the ready-mix lorry, and the concrete was pumped over the wall through a flexible pipe from College Street. The architect, Michael Carden, recalls that this caused considerable difficulty because of the unusual length of pipe: a man standing on the Close wall acted as link between the lorry and those manning the delivery end of the tube, but there were anxious moments when the joints in the pipe gave way, spewing concrete everywhere. There was a sad sequel. After the architect had left, the builders decided to pump into the river the water lying in the trenches above the concrete, thus putting paid to fishing downstream for the entire season.

The new teaching block, a three-storey building in Wealden Brick, contained five main rooms. On the ground floor were the Maths and English Rooms, and on the first floor, the Science and French Rooms, whose layout was designed by the respective Heads of Department. The old Science Room in the Salwey extension became a specialist History Room, while the old French Room became a

XXVI Old Pilgrims gathered around the newly-opened Selwyn building, 5 October 1974. In front of right-hand window: Humphrey Salwey, Margie Briggs, Martin Briggs, Lorna Salwey

XXVII June 1977. The Queen's Silver Jubilee. Archbishop Donald Coggan presents two sets of J Block twins (Jonathan and Jeremy Large; Andrew and Stephen Brill) to Her Majesty the Queen, during a visit to Lambeth Palace with Ann Coggan

reasonably large Music Room, where chamber music could take place, and small-scale choral activities. On the top floor of the new block was a sizeable Art Room contained under an elegant mansard roof. The building was designed so that it could be extended northwards if necessary, by building a mirror image of the block on the other side of the stairwell. This accounts for the building's rather squat present appearance.

Work went ahead with remarkable speed, and the topping-out ceremony was held on 20 June 1974. After several weeks of hard work during the summer holidays, when £850 worth of fittings and equipment paid for by The Pilgrims' School Society was installed, the building was ready for the first lessons of the Christmas term.

The name of the new block was the subject of heated discussion. At first, it was proposed that it should be called the 'Nicholas Building', after the Warden of Winchester College to whom the external appearance of the oldest part of the school buildings is largely due; but some felt that he already had his memorial in those very buildings. Finally, the block was named the 'Selwyn Building', in honour of the late Dean whose vision had brought the school into being.

The second stage of the development which the Headmaster had outlined, the provision of new Music Rooms, would not take place for some years, and would require a second appeal. In spite of the impressive sums raised in 1972, nobody could have foreseen the alarming rise in building costs during the two years that elapsed before the work was completed, and no further funds were available. Thus Martin Briggs had regretfully to write: 'The Music Rooms must come, but not yet'.

As we have seen, the success of the Appeal was largely due to the enthusiastic efforts of the parents. The Parents' Association was formed as a sub-committee of the Pilgrims' School Society in June 1972, and became a separate body four years later: its aims were 'to help the school in any way found possible or suitable, and to arrange meetings of general interest for parents'. The first such meeting took place in the Pilgrims' Hall the following October, when three Public School headmasters: John Thorn of Winchester, Dennis Silk of Radley and Roger Griffiths of Hurstpierpoint, answered questions sent in beforehand by parents. The following year the first 'Subject Evenings' were held: the Science and Maths departments were host to a group of parents, who became the pupils of Margot Meredith, David Cheetham and Frank Skipwith for a short while, thus gaining insight into the methods used to instruct their sons.

Equally important were the 'Block Evenings' instituted in 1973, when parents were given an opportunity of meeting all those who taught their sons, and discussing their progress. Martin Briggs felt that it was important to monitor the academic progress of the large number of boys in the school as effectively as possible, and a system of 'assessments' had been created whereby parents were informed of their sons' progress three or four times a term.

Despite the loyal support given by Deputy Headmaster, Secretary and staff, running such a complex school as The Pilgrims' was inevitably a full-time occupation for a schoolmaster with such uncompromising views of his pastoral responsibilities as Martin Briggs; and during term-time, his family had to take second place. Perhaps these considerations were foremost in bringing about his decision to try a different way of life while his children were still growing up.

Thus at the end of the Christmas term 1974 Martin and Margie Briggs announced their retirement from schoolmastering; Martin had been appointed administrator of an important National Trust property, Cotehele House, in Cornwall. And so the Dean and Chapter found itself seeking a new Headmaster for the second time in five years. Meanwhile the life of the school continued smoothly: there was a production of *A Midsummer Night's Dream* and an unprecedented number of musical events involving Choristers, Quiristers and Commoners alike. Shortly after the beginning of the summer term of 1975, it was announced that Stephen McWatters, formerly Headmaster of Clifton College, had been elected Headmaster of The Pilgrims' School.

Stephen McWatters took up his appointment at the beginning of January 1976: he and his wife Mary had been living in Winchester since the summer, teaching part-time at Winchester College and making valuable contacts there.

His first year passed quietly enough. In July 1976 Chris Hazelgrove, who had run the Art Department for eight years, was compelled to retire through ill-health. Her enthusiastic work was continued by Marjory Monro, who had previously taught at The Pilgrims' for three years, and who rejoined the staff as Head of Art and form teacher.

The year was notable, also, for the double dramatic production of the Christmas term 1976: W. S. Gilbert's *Rosencrantz and Guildenstern* and Britten's *The Little Sweep*. The opera all but overshadowed the playlet, and rehearsals involving an unprecedented number of boys (for a double cast was selected, as in previous school productions) continued for more than three months. One sad coincidence was the death of the composer during the weeks immediately preceding the final performances, and a letter of sympathy from the cast brought a touching reply from Sir Peter Pears.

Clement McWilliam was the master-mind behind this venture, and at the same time was pressing for the Appeal to be re-opened in order to provide funds to build the long awaited Music Practice Rooms. After months of preparation, the Music Room Appeal was launched in March 1977 under Clement McWilliam's direction, with secretarial help from Celia Salwey and ex-Chorister John Ford. Trusts were approached, and two responded generously, with gifts totalling £3,000. Money was raised by means of concerts, recitals in the Cathedral and at the College, talks, silver-foil collections – not to mention the Nestlés' 'fund-raising chocolate scheme', which made a profit of over £200 during the first year of its existence! The Pilgrims' School Society contributed £1,500 towards instruments. In September 1978, nearly a year after the Rooms were completed, a sponsored walk, organised by Keith Ross and involving the whole school, closed the Appeal, bringing in a final £2,500.

During the summer choir-time of 1977 Choristers sat on the curved wall of the Lockburn, in a half-hearted protest against the imminent destruction of the ancient watercourse. The bulldozers arrived after the end of choir-time, however, and the boys' efforts were of no avail. In fact, the building operation merely involved covering over the last visible portion of the old stream created by Ethelwold, 'maker of the conduits', and the Lockburn still flows beneath the practice rooms.

Like the Selwyn Building, the new Music Rooms were a compromise between practical necessity and the need to preserve an attractive corner of the Cathedral Close. Stephen McWatters described it thus:

> The new Music Block has an ingenuity and complexity of design – a complexity, like so much else at Pilgrims', out of all proportion to its size – dictated by the need to fit it into a very limited space while still keeping the roof low; to present a blank front to the playground while admitting enough light; and to harmonise with the existing buildings.

Whatever the aesthetic merits of the design, there can be no doubting the practical success of the Block, which provided the school with five practice rooms of various shapes and sizes and a certain amount of space for the storage of instruments and music.

The Rooms were opened on 15 December 1977 by Angus Watson, Master of the Music of Winchester College. In a short speech, Mr. Watson described how he would plan an ideal school: Music Rooms first, then dining room facilities and classrooms much later! He cut the red ribbon; the Band gave an energetic rendering of the 'British Grenadiers'. Celebrations continued throughout the afternoon and evening, with two performances of a Concert, and a Christmas tea; and the day finished with an appropriate bang when Clement McWilliam sent up a monster rocket.

The year 1977 saw another innovation: the first 'Pilgrims' Services' on occasional Sunday mornings. Until that date, Commoner boarders had attended Mattins in the Cathedral every Sunday, but it was now felt appropriate to provide a religious service aimed at the particular needs of the younger congregation, especially on the so-called 'Liturgy' days, when the Cathedral services took the form of a combined Mattins and Communion service. The first School Service was held in St Lawrence's Church in May 1977, by kind permission of the Reverend Trevor Nash. Following a fire at St Lawrence's the services were transferred to our own Pilgrims' Hall, where they have been held ever since. A feature of School Services has been the choice of preacher: generally a lay-man selected for his ability to hold the attention of a youthful congregation.

Early in 1978 the Choir set off for Paris on the first of a series of foreign trips. At Charles de Gaulle airport Clergy, Lay Clerks and Choristers were met by a 'worker priest', in moderate control of an antiquated single-decker 'bus. There was some doubt as to whether the Choir would be safely transported to Meudon in time for the first recital, but despite a brush with a *deux-chevaux* and several near misses involving more formidable opposition, the Choristers arrived unscathed. The two recitals in the suburbs were poorly attended, but this seemed to matter little. The boys slept in one corner of a vast dormitory in an orphanage, a room seemingly the size of our Cathedral, with towering Corinthian pillars and bathroom facilities which were more than quaintly antique. Next day, the Choir sang Evensong in Notre-Dame Cathedral, the first Anglican choir to do so. The event was reckoned a resounding success, despite some difficulties with demonstrators, who let off *pétards* during the service – it was never quite clear whether religious grievances were involved.

The Kitsons spent the following term and the summer holidays on well-earned sabbatical leave at Arisaig, Scotland. Jim Hobson looked after 'Q School', and

Dick's Main School activities were shared among other members of staff. His administrative duties were undertaken by Frank Skipwith. This provided, no doubt, useful practice in running a school, for a few months later, in December 1978, Frank left The Pilgrims' to become headmaster of Fernden School, near Haslemere. He was succeeded as Head of Mathematics by Captain Stuart Roberts, who had joined the staff in September 1977 after a successful career in the Royal Navy.

The postman in Dick and Islay's Scottish retreat must have been astonished at the volume of correspondence addressed to them, not least by the boys who thus discharged their Sunday letter-writing duty. Amongst one morning's receipt was this letter from John Baker:

Dear Dick and Islay,
So glad you are having a restful time, as indeed we are. The slight fire only destroyed Dorm I and I think we lost only two boys (their names escape me now). The drain blockage in the back garden has caused the loss of a few plants only, and the men promise to fill in the trench *before* November if all goes well. Kingsgate Street was opened up last Tuesday and some minor superficial damage was caused to the Day-room by the bulldozer, but we got it out before prep and have put polythene sheet in the window-spaces, which are now quite draught-free really. It's surprising how much rain has seeped in through Dorm II ceiling: it's been so wet, hasn't it? A large tin bath has been lent us by the Deanery, and the boys find sleeping in swimming trunks quite fun. I expect the change will do them good. Tusa i and Stamenkovic have mild typhoid, I hear, but we are assured it will not spread. That's about all in a particularly uneventful not to say humdrum term. All good wishes and don't worry about a thing.   J.K.B.

P.S. We had kidneys for supper & I was sick again.

The year 1977 had produced the highest crop of scholarships for many years, including the first and second music awards at Winchester, the top music scholarship at Sherborne and the top academic scholarship to Shrewsbury. After several years of only average performance, attributable no doubt to continuing problems caused by the expansion of the school, The Pilgrims' seemed to be recovering its former academic reputation. Two important contributory factors were the careful monitoring of academic progress by means of 'Assessments' – a system devised by Martin Briggs – and the re-distribution of 'A Block' boys into first- and second-year forms established by Stephen McWatters.

The Choir's short trip to Paris had given Choristers and Lay Clerks a certain insight into the problems of international travel: above all, the difficulties of transporting cassocks, surplices, music, publicity material and all the *impedimenta* of the Church Music business. However, this modest excursion was insignificant compared with the mammoth venture of February-March 1979, when The Pilgrims' School found itself without 17 Choristers, the indefatigable Head Matron, Miss Ellis-Jones, and the Lay Clerk masters, including the author, during a 23-day Choir Tour of North America: the opening musical event of the Cathedral's 900th anniversary celebrations.

All had to be meticulously planned, from the knitting of the Choir's red, woolly hats and the fitting of warm clothing to beat Canada's sub-zero temperatures (−29°F in Ottawa!) to the photocopying of the music which would be sung at over 13 services and 15 concerts, not to mention recording sessions and TV appearances. There were concerts in the National Arts Centre of Canada, in Washington's new Kennedy Center and in the Carnegie Hall; recitals at the two university towns of Princeton and Harvard within 24 hours; an Evensong in the cathedral of St John the Divine, New York, the biggest church in the world; as well as a Eucharist in the modest parish church of Winchester, Massachusetts (it was a disappointment to learn that this little Boston suburb was named not after our cathedral city but the rifle). Altogether we stayed in seven major cities and were variously billeted in schools, theological colleges, retreat centres and private houses. It was a trip memorable for the lavish hospitality of our American hosts and the evident appreciation of congregations and audiences.

Many and various were the experiences of the Choristers, some of whose activities were relayed to parents and friends in England via a telex link. There were the electrically-charged sandwiches at the residence of the Governor-General in Ottawa; the questionable tact of singing *Vive la Canadienne!* in French at the same gathering; the unforgettable sight of the frozen Niagara Falls during a time of record cold; the noisy visit to the steel-rolling mill; the ice-floes swirling down the Potomac River in Washington. Few boys will ever forget the opulent accommodation provided by the good citizens of Shaker Heights, just outside bankrupt Cleveland. Then there was the food: the huge breakfasts at Ashbury College, Ottawa, and the delights of do-it-yourself rotary toasters; those curious sausages accompanied by pancakes and dripping with maple syrup, on the plane between Cleveland and Cincinnati; and the monster hamburgers consumed during a motorway stop south of Boston.

Inevitably there were set-backs and difficulties: we abandoned a boy in Ottawa's science museum; got stuck in the snow at Niagara; lost our way in the bus many times in the New York suburbs; and found ourselves without an organ, an hour before the start of the Carnegie Hall concert. Yet none of these problems proved insuperable, and Choristers and adults returned to England physically exhausted, but enriched by a testing experience that made them the envy of their colleagues who had stayed at home.

A few weeks after their return from the New World, the Choristers were joined in the Cathedral by the Children of the Chapel Royal for that most English of ceremonies, the distribution of the Royal Maundy. Equally closely involved were two local 'Children of the Almonry', Commoner Philip Baldwin and Quirister sister Emma Smith, who accompanied Her Majesty during the distribution. Although Maundy Thursday fell during the holidays, about 60 Pilgrims' School boys assembled in the Close to watch the Queen leave the Deanery.

The Choristers were kept busy during the Cathedral's 900th Anniversary celebrations, with concerts in Winchester, Bournemouth, Oxford and Cheltenham. No less busy were the Quiristers, who acted in a new Winchester College production of Purcell's *King Arthur*. The Pilgrims' contribution to this opera was considerable: six Old Boys played in the orchestra, 10 sang in the chorus, and major parts were taken by Old Pilgrims Mark Salter, James Simpson and Andrew Tusa.

During the Choir's American trip, the significant burden of looking after the physical well-being of increasingly exhausted Choristers had fallen on Miss Thelma Ellis-Jones, the Head Matron. She retired from this post at the end of the summer, and was replaced by Mary Taylor, trained at the prestigious Norland Nursery Training College. Mary had worked in a co-educational international preparatory school in Kenya and was to introduce many generations of Pilgrims' boys to the magic of Africa. She encouraged practical help to the world's needy by organising annual bring-and-buy sales, and formed a popular Naturewatch club. Under Mary's enthusiastic leadership the Matrons' department has become, as never before, a fully integrated part of school life. The work-room is not just a place where boys resort when unwell, but a haven where those wanting friendly adult company, or advice when in any sort of difficulty at school or home, can be sure of finding a friendly ear. At the same time, the permanent Music Staff was doubled with the arrival of Miss Hilary Brooks, a baroque music specialist and experienced general musician, whose chamber recitals with the ensemble *Ancient Lights* became a regular feature of The Pilgrims' musical life.

Early in September 1979, five days before the beginning of term, the Cathedral Choir gave a performance of sacred works from the cathedral repertoire at a Promenade Concert, broadcast from St Augustine's Church, Kilburn: a rare privilege for a provincial choir and a sign of the rising reputation of Winchester's cathedral singers.

The ensuing academic year was notable for its performance of *Julius Caesar*, produced by Stephen McWatters. It was a long time before the stains of blood from Caesar's 30 wounds faded from the Pilgrims' Hall stage.

The summer term 1980 marked the end of an era: it was the final term of Dick Kitson's 17th year as Deputy Headmaster. During that time he had also taught a full timetable, run the Classics department, edited the *Pilgrims' School Magazine*, acted as Secretary to the Pilgrims' School Society, coached games, and looked after the Romans Set; quite apart from his out-of-school work as secretary to the 'Hampshire Hoggets', organising some 15 to 20 cricket matches each summer for 13- to 19-year-olds. Dick maintained his responsibility for Quiristers' School, but handed over the deputy headmastership to Keith Ross, who quickly mastered the intricacies of time-tabling, the compiling of the 'weekly notice', and the smooth running of the complex Pilgrims' machine.

No doubt the Cathedral Choir's success at the Proms led to their being invited to give the opening concert of the City of London Festival, in St Bartholomew's Church, Smithfield. The Choristers received a warm welcome from the incumbent, the Revd. Arthur Brown, a former Winchester Chorister and the son of Mr. Stawell Brown, who had created the school lantern slide collection in the early Thirties. It was an appropriate coincidence on the eve of the school's 50th year.

Preparations for the Golden Jubilee occupied almost 12 months, though some care was taken to ensure that this momentous event did not interfere overmuch with school routine. The Choristers had other things to occupy them: first, a two-day trip to the Channel Islands in October 1980, where they fitted in two recitals, a short television programme, and a visit to Gerald Durrell's Zoo; then a slightly longer stay in Sweden during the 1981 February Half-Term break. The social high-spot of this tour was a buffet lunch at the British Embassy in Stockholm, followed by an impromptu skating session: in a moment of post-prandial euphoria the Organist raced seawards over the melting ice, followed by 18 Choristers. They were mere dots in a white landscape when the Master in charge of Choristers and the Matron arrived and noticed the warning signs.

Less hazardous were the activities of the Quiristers, now under the direction of Julian Smith following Raymond Humphrey's retirement in September 1979. They took part in an increasing number of 'outside' events: some sang in a Thames Television competition, *Fanfare for Young Musicians*, and all of them gave charity recitals at Fernhill, an old people's home in Chandler's Ford, and at Beech House, near Reading. Just before Christmas 1980 they were joined by members of the Commoners' Choir and 33 other adult singers, mostly staff and parents, for a performance of Vaughan Williams's *Hodie* in the Chapel of St Cross, conducted by Clement McWilliam.

In March 1981 there was a major event in the Cathedral: two performances of *Passion and Resurrection*, a dramatic oratorio by the contemporary English composer Jonathan Harvey, who at that time had a son in the Cathedral Choir. Bishop John Taylor produced this demanding work, and the entire undertaking – rehearsals and performance – was filmed by the BBC. The cast included eight Choristers, who took the part of angels; Jeremy Clayre and Nicholas Vellacott acted as thurifers; and John Crook was one of the crucified thieves.

During the Easter holidays 1981 the school premises were enlarged with the incorporation of Cheyney Court as the headmaster's house. Interestingly, this fine Tudor building, once part of the bishop's courthouse, had for a time during the 19th century accommodated the Quiristers, under the headmastership of William Whiting. Keith Ross, as Deputy Headmaster, now moved into the flat in Main School.

Choir tours apart, the school began to provide increasing opportunities for foreign travel. For some years Jim and Liz Hobson took parties of boys from The Pilgrims' and from Twyford School on the Mediterranean Cruises organised by the I.A.P.S. aboard S.S. *Uganda* – until that ship was requisitioned during the Falklands Crisis and ultimately scrapped. Frank Skipwith was the first to organise the annual school ski trips that for many are still a highlight of the Easter holidays. And for several years Clement McWilliam, accompanied in turn by Ambrose Streatfeild and Keith Ross, hired a longboat and covered vast tracts of England's inland waterways in the company of groups of Pilgrims past and present.

The main Jubilee celebrations occupied the weekend of 10-12 July 1981. Preparations had gone on for months. There had been special staff meetings; Old Pilgrims' address lists had meticulously been checked; John Baker, assisted by boy helpers, had printed brochures, booking forms and tickets on the school press; and John Crook had consumed many a pint of midnight oil compiling the first edition of the *History of The Pilgrims' School*. The load on the teaching staff was lightened by the temporary appointment of Jonathan Thomson-Glover, a promising young Modern Languages student in his 'gap year' between Clifton and London University. Even so, a great burden fell on the shoulders of Clement McWilliam, who was responsible for co-ordinating the celebrations.

On 9 July a huge marquee was erected on the back lawn, and we realised that the Jubilee was upon us. The entire Selwyn building was given over to exhibitions. Art and Science projects were displayed, and in the French Room guests were

XXVIII 11 July 1981. Golden Jubilee celebrations. Dick Kitson, Clement McWilliam, Keith Ross, Stephen McWatters, Mary McWatters, Lorna Salwey, Humphrey Salwey, John Crook

XXIX After an exhibition tennis match during the Jubilee celebrations. Stephen McWatters, Martin Hillier, Jamie Byng, Jonathan Thomson Glover

able to study photographs of school life and watch a continuous projection of colour slides of the Choristers' foreign tours. In the Maths Room, Captain Roberts organised a display by the Model Club, which included a Meccano replica of a crane in Portsmouth Dockyard, loading and unloading cargo into a seven-foot-long model of a Royal Fleet Auxiliary, all by remote control. The English Room was turned into the Jubilee Shop, selling Jubilee mugs, cards and prints of the school, and copies of the school *History*. There were further displays in the Quiet Room and front hall, and the History Room was given over to an exhibition of photographs illustrating the history of the school since 1931.

At 4.00 p.m. everyone made their way to the Cathedral for Evensong, sung by a choir made up of Choristers, Quiristers and Commoners, the lower parts being taken by members of staff, parents, Old Pilgrims and some Lay Clerks. The service consisted of Psalm 15, the Magnificat and Nunc Dimittis by Stanford in B flat (with orchestral accompaniment), and Bairstow's anthem *Blessed City*. Clement McWilliam directed proceedings, and had written a special hymn for the occasion, to the tune *Gonfalon Royal*. The sermon was preached by the Bishop of Wakefield, the Rt. Revd. Colin James, who at that time had a son in the school.

Later that evening about 100 old boys and some members of staff sat down to an Old Pilgrims' Dinner in the marquee. John Hunter, the senior O.P. present, proposed the health of the guests: Humphrey Salwey, Martin Briggs and Stephen McWatters. Humphrey Salwey, rising to respond, had to wait for several minutes before the loud applause and repeated choruses of *For He's a Jolly Good Fellow* died down. Reminiscing about the early history of the school, he wished it the best of health and prosperity for the next 50 years.

Paradoxically, the boarders were wakened at the habitual early hour next morning, despite the noisy interruptions to their sleep, while the dayboys came to school much later than usual. Lessons were abandoned, and swimming races took place at the College pool between mixed teams of Old Pilgrims and current pupils. At lunchtime old boys and staff met in the marquee, while parents and boys ate picnic lunches on Wolvesey field. The weather, which had seemed somewhat unpromising during the morning, gradually improved, and an exhibition cricket match between two teams of O.P.s, reinforced by a few members of the First XI, took place in glorious sunshine. From 3.45 there was tea for all in the marquee – some 700 people – during which a Promenade Orchestra conducted by Hilary Brooks played in the Pilgrims' Hall. After Evensong, attended by many Old Pilgrims, there was the third performance of an opera written for the occasion by Clement McWilliam, *The Two Singers* (based on a short story by Turgenev, adapted by Winchester College don, Michael Fontes), and a concert in College Music School by Quiristers past and present.

During the following week two sherry parties were held: one for music teachers, former members of staff, and friends of the school, together with representatives of local firms with a close connection with the school, and the other for our own catering, domestic and maintenance staff.

Finally, the celebrations were brought to a close with a Jubilee Dance organised by the Pilgrims' School Society. There was dancing in the dining room and in the senior classroom, supper in the Pilgrims' Hall and a bar and sitting-out tables in the marquee. It was an appropriately stylish close to the school's 50th year.

Chapter Ten

THE NEXT TEN YEARS

SCARCELY HAD THE JUBILEE marquee been dismantled than a team of builders moved in to start work on an extension of the school premises that would be made of more solid stuff than canvas. At ground floor level this affected the changing rooms, whose size was virtually doubled with the addition of an area for the juniors; on the first floor a new dormitory, sick room and utility room were created, together with a bed-sitting room and bathroom for the Head Matron and a guest room. A new corridor ran from the Common Room to the matrons' domain. Clement McWilliam acted as link man between the school and the builders, giving up a large part of his holidays. His expertise in plumbing, electrical wiring and drainage proved invaluable.

The changes in the environment were matched by changes in personnel. At the end of the 1981 summer term Jim Hobson had left The Pilgrims' to take control of Beaconhurst Grange School near Stirling, the sixth Pilgrims' master in 12 years to become a headmaster. He was replaced by Jeremy Edwards, whose ancient motor cars, with a petrol consumption commensurate with their faded luxury, became a familiar feature of the Cathedral Close. Two other new members of the teaching staff – at first on a part-time basis – were Allan Mottram (who had come to Winchester as a Lay Clerk and was to leave it as a choir school headmaster) and Marian Tewkesbury; both were to become long-serving full members of the school community. A sponsored walk, organised by the indefatigable Keith Ross shortly after the start of the new academic year, provided an ideal opportunity for boys and new staff to get to know one another and raised nearly £3,000 for the Mayor of Winchester's Christmas Fund for the Disabled.

This was an exciting time for the Quiristers. In October eight of them were televised in Thames Television's competition for children under the age of 13, *Fanfare for Young Musicians*, as Dick Kitson recalls:

Julian Smith had made for them a three-part arrangement of Schubert's *Nacht und Träume*, to be sung in German with piano accompaniment. By 25th November, when the programme which included the Quiristers was broadcast, we knew that they were one of the four groups selected for the final, from an initial field of 199. So on 4th December they went off to the Teddington studios once again, this time staying the night in a hotel, where they made full use of the facilities. The following day they made the recording. And at the end of the programme, when the results were announced in the usual reverse order, the looks on the faces of the eight boys as it slowly dawned on them that there was no one else left to take first place was quite a study.

Not to be outdone, the Choristers appeared in a light-hearted Christmas programme featuring Rolf Harris, and a vulpine side-kick, Basil Brush. In April 1982 the Cathedral Choir set off for their second transatlantic tour, to western Canada this time. It turned out that this was the first visit by an English choir to these parts for nearly 60 years. Our antics were wired by to England by telex:

Howdy folks, here we are in Calgary, after a long but tolerable flight. This morning to cathedral, and rehearse a few notes to show we are genuine, then to Elkana ranch for the day. On approaching, attacked by outlaw bandits with guns. They capture chorister hostage, and offer to string him high in nearest tree. We are offered bear steaks. It is another world.

. . . Then to aquarium, where we see killer whales doing their routines. At right places in commentary they demonstrate their teeth, tails, flippers, singing voices, and leaping from water. They are very biddable and sing beautifully. Martin must think he would rather run a whale park than a cathedral choir.

. . . The concert at the Orpheum, Edmonton, is sold out, with queues at the door, and our programme is received with exceptional enthusiasm. Critic writes in paper: 'The most beautiful thing in the world is to hear an English cathedral choir'.

The following letter, received by the author some months after our return to England, tells its own sad story of the loss during the tour of a much-loved cuddly toy:

Dear Mr. Crook,
This letter is in regard to your letter of April 26, 1982. We are sorry to say that the teddy bear 'PAWS' was not to be found anywhere on the Complex. Hopefully the owner will be able to adjust to this mishap. However, if the teddy bear is found we will keep your address on file so as to return it to you promptly.
Sincerely,
Charlene Rooney
(Secretary, National Panasonic Tower,
Niagara Falls, Canada).

Meanwhile, four boys had set off with Jim Hobson for the annual I.A.P.S. Mediterranean cruise aboard *Uganda*. Within a few days the vessel had been commandeered by the Government to serve as a hospital ship during the Falklands Crisis. Thus all the passengers were put ashore at Naples after steaming at full speed from Alexandria. Ever to the fore, the three children (out of a passenger list of 944) to be interviewed by the BBC after leaving the ship were Pilgrims' boys.

In 1982 Winchester College celebrated its 600th anniversary, an exciting time for the Quiristers. As members of the original foundation, they lined up with the

College men to receive the Queen *Ad Portas*. On her way out, Her Majesty, joined by the Duke of Edinburgh, who had landed on Meads by helicopter, graciously addressed a word or two to some of them. The Quiristers also took part in a festival performance of *Fidelio*, staged in Winchester College New Hall.

The Pilgrims' School's major dramatic event of 1982 was a performance of *A Midsummer Night's Dream*, produced by the Headmaster and reviewed in style by a young C-Blocker for his English prep:

A Midsummer Night's Dream was written by William Shakespeare in about the 16th century. Shakespeare was a very famous writer then. This play is one of his comedies, and it is very famous too. I think that the Mechanicals were the best, because they were *so* funny, and I have an eye to enjoy comedies as well. Once they did a play in front of a Duke that was *so* funny. I think I'll write about that play tonight.

Fisby was in love with Bottom: she wore the most idiotic wig you ever saw, and waved her head proudly whenever her name was mentioned. One man was a tower – well, supposed to be – and one had a dog and a lantern. I've forgotten both their names. The lantern was supposed to be the Moon. And there was Snug, too – he was thick – in their little play he was a lion. He came into the play when Fisby had just come on alone. He growled behind Fisby and she went off screaming. Then Bottom came on saying, 'I must die, die, die'. The way he said it made it very funny indeed. Fisby came on again and saw Bottom and said, 'I must die, die, die': she was even funnier.
P.S. I'm not sure whether the woman in the play was called Fisby or not.

At the end of the school year, following the success of the Jubilee celebrations, an O.P. Day was organised, attended by over 40 old boys of various ages. Lorna Salwey planted a Whitebeam near the river to mark, somewhat belatedly, the school's Golden Jubilee.

During the ensuing holidays the Cathedral Choir and Waynflete Singers performed Bach's *Magnificat* in a Promenade Concert at the Royal Albert Hall under the direction of Martin Neary. A notable feature of this event was that the chorus included no fewer than nine members of the teaching staff and one member of the Governing Body, Canon Job.

At our return to school in September 1982 some wondered whether a new member of staff had arrived unannounced when the initials 'MH' appeared on the timetable. They turned out to refer to Margaret Morris, who had married Mr. Martin Henderson during the summer months. Margaret continued teaching for two further terms until she took her retirement to have a baby daughter. She was succeeded as form mistress of JM, conveniently enough, by another 'MH', Mrs. Margaret Humphrys. Also in 1983 Dick Kitson celebrated 75 terms of schoolmastering at The Pilgrims', and at the end of the summer term he and Islay retired from Q-School. Colin and Leslie Thompson, who had previously lived at Domum Lodge, a little way up Kingsgate Street, now took over the running of Quiristers' School, and Nigel Kinloch was appointed Master in charge of Dayboys.

The year 1982–3 was notable for two major musical productions. Early in December Clement McWilliam produced for the second time Britten's *Let's Make an Opera!*, rewriting Act I to make it more relevant to life at The Pilgrims'. Thus the adult members of the cast at first played themselves: Ken Tewkesbury staggered on stage under the weight of a pile of unmarked exercise books; Allan Mottram arrived late for a rehearsal because of the long psalms for the 15th Evening in the Cathedral; Hilary Brooks was recovering from a hard day's music teaching; and Clement himself was, in the play, persuaded to write and direct *The Little Sweep*, the opera of the main title. Daniel Daukes and Thomas Crawford took the part of Sammy the Sweep on alternate nights, supported by excellent acting from other junior members of the cast, and from one guest adult singer, Rachel Firth, in the guise of the evil Miss Baggott. The opera will long be remembered as one of Clement McWilliam's most inspired dramatic events.

The second production was another locally-written opera, *Robin Hood*, by Ken Gross and James Sabben-Clare, with music by Robert Bottone. Like *The Little Sweep*, the opera seemed to grow out of an everyday situation. The Quiristers were portrayed at choir practice being urged by their conductor, Julian Smith, to put more enthusiasm into their singing of *Under the Greenwood Tree*. They fell to imagining life in Sherwood Forest, and soon all were participating in the colour and excitement of the Robin Hood story.

The early 1980s witnessed the first, tentative beginnings of what was eventually to become a major, timetabled school subject. The *Pilgrims' School Magazine* for 1981 had noted the purchase of a 'microcomputer', which to most of us at the time seemed little more than an entertaining toy. Thanks to the enthusiasm of Captain Stuart Roberts an appeal was soon launched for five Sinclair ZX81 computers. Parents kindly provided redundant black and white television sets to serve as monitors. By 1983 eight computer terminals had been wired up in the Maths Room by Captain Roberts, assisted by a parent, Mr. Chesters. The system was arranged so that a single tape recorder could load a program into all eight computers at once, and forms from the B Block upwards enjoyed at least one period of 'computer-assisted learning' each week. The following year a BBC 'B' computer was installed in the Science Room, the ZX81s were replaced by Sir Clive Sinclair's new *Spectrum* models, and we began to dream of a computer room. This dream was of course eventually realised – Nigel Kinloch was appointed Head of Computer Studies in 1987 and the History Room became the Computer Centre.

At Easter 1982 Stephen McWatters had announced his intention of retiring as Headmaster at the end of the following year, and in July 1983 he and Mary moved to their house in Edgar Road. During nearly eight years in office he had been responsible for two major building projects and had steered the school through the Cathedral's 900th anniversary celebrations, the Pilgrims' own Golden Jubilee and the 600th anniversary of Winchester College. During that time academic standards had continued to improve, as had sporting achievements: Stephen himself, a keen sportsman, was often to be found coaching junior rugby or taking some of the older boys to a squash session at the Winchester College courts, quite apart from his teaching of Classics. Mary McWatters had taught junior French and coached the seniors in French conversation. In a tribute published in the *Pilgrims' School Magazine* Dick Kitson emphasised Stephen's encouragement of music:

Music in the school has expanded enormously, so that now about 120 out of 168 boys are learning at least one instrument and there have been many first-rate concerts in the last seven years: in some of these Stephen has trained his own group of instrumentalists. As members of the Waynflete Singers and Music Club, moreover, he and Mary have taken part in a number of concerts which have involved the Choristers and Quiristers as well.

Stephen McWatters was succeeded in September 1983 by Michael Kefford. For the new Headmaster this was in many ways a return to old haunts: his grandfather had been rector of Shaw-cum-Donnington, near Newbury, and his father for many years had been headmaster of Edinburgh House School, New Milton. Michael Kefford had taught at Edinburgh House, then at West Downs. After six years as a housemaster in a co-educational school in Croydon he was appointed headmaster of Colston's preparatory school, Bristol, where he spent nine years. Michael and Elizabeth Kefford and their two children, Rupert and Alison, moved into Cheyney Court early in August, a month before the start of the new school year.

From the outset Michael Kefford's Christian commitment was evident. He made it clear how much value he placed on the morning Assemblies, at which the entire school gathered for a reading, a short talk, and prayers in the Pilgrims' Hall: 'perhaps the most important thing we do all term', as he himself described it. A Lay Reader, he was quickly pressed into service in the Cathedral, and his wide range of contacts ensured a steady supply of suitable preachers for the increasing number of School Services in the Pilgrims' Hall. These services provided the opportunity for boys, parents and staff to join in Sunday worship in a family atmosphere, complementing the more formal traditions of worship in the Cathedral.

An energetic sportsman, the new Headmaster was anxious that The Pilgrims' School should maintain, and even build on, its already excellent record on the games field. In this he was fortunate in having the support of superb coaches in so many sports: the devoted cricket coaching of Ambrose Streatfeild and Dick Kitson; Colin Thompson's involvement in all school sports, particularly soccer and athletics; Keith Ross's enthusiastic coaching of First XI Hockey; and Stuart Roberts' expertise in laying the foundations for sporting success with the junior boys.

Also evident at an early stage was Michael Kefford's wish that the school premises should be as pleasant as possible. In this he was ably seconded by Bursar David Feast, a former R.A.F. officer who joined the school in January 1984, replacing the popular Freddie Hargreaves and our long-serving bursarial assistant, Mrs. Pat Bright. Year by year, the *School Magazine* catalogued the improvements: a complete programme of redecoration inside and out, and the eventual carpeting of every classroom in the school.

In these aims Michael Kefford was supported by his wife Elizabeth, who took over the supervision of domestic arrangements, helped out in the matrons' department at times of crisis, organised match teas, and acted as a sympathetic link between the school and the parents.

In the Cathedral, the summer term of 1984 was notable for its 'Saxon Festival', commemorating the 1000th anniversary of the death of Ethelwold, the Anglo-Saxon bishop who had reformed Old Minster as a Benedictine Priory and enlarged

XXX Parents' Association picnic, 1988. Michael Kefford with Lord and Lady Denning at The Lawns, Whitchurch

XXXI Timothy Barber presents a prizewinning picture of the picnic to Lord Denning, 19 June 1988

XXXII The annual cricket match between the Choristers and the Dean and Chapter, July 1986. Back row: Canon Alec Wedderspoon, Michael Kefford, Michael Manktelow (Bp. of Basingstoke), Keith Ross, Dean Michael Stancliffe, Canon Roger Job, David Feast, Colin Hick (Lay Clerk 'stiffening'), Rupert Kefford, Canon Paul Britton, Ray Godfrey (Custos), Robert Sherwin (scorer)

the monastery church, predecessor of our present Cathedral. A special Liturgy to mark the opening of the Festival included a performance of the *Quem Quaeritis* drama from the *Winchester Troper*, in a new edition prepared for us by Dr. Susan Rankin. Canon Job took the part of the Angel, and the three Maries, who made a spectacular entrance in clouds of incense, were represented – somewhat improbably – by Lay Clerks, including Allan Mottram and John Crook.

Another highlight of the summer term was the picnic organised by the Parents' Association in the idyllic setting of Lord and Lady Denning's house by the River Test at Whitchurch, a gathering that was to become an annual event. Various games were organised on the spacious lawns, Lord and Lady Denning wandered around the groups chatting to boys, parents and staff, and the afternoon ended in a tug-of-war, in which members of the losing team were dragged to a watery fate.

In mid-July the Cathedral Choir sang in a concert in Burghclere parish church, part of a private music festival organised by Andrew Lloyd Webber, who lived nearby. He had written a special piece for the occasion, a setting of the Requiem Mass. At the time we were quite unaware of the impact that this piece was to have on our lives.

Michael Kefford's first year as Headmaster was marked by a notable triumph on the academic front: William Chesters had been placed at the Head of the Roll in the Winchester College Election examinations, the third such success in the history of the school. This was a splendid achievement for the Headmaster to be able to mention in his Speech Day report.

He expressed thanks to those experienced members of the school staff who had helped him settle into his new school, singling out in particular Dick Kitson, with his unrivalled knowledge of every aspect of Pilgrims' life; Keith Ross, the Deputy Headmaster, who shouldered the burden of the everyday running of the school; and Rosemary Poole, who, as secretary both to the school and the headmaster, worked so efficiently and cheerfully – answering the telephone with never-failing courtesy, answering parental enquiries, dealing with new boy entries and voice trials, typing hundreds of letters and lists every week, and yet finding time to get to know personally every boy in the school.

At the same time, he paid tribute to Jane Stear, who had unfortunately been obliged to give up teaching in the middle of the summer term as a result of ill-health. A year later, on O.P. Day, 14 July 1985, a presentation was made to Jane by the many Old Pilgrims who remembered her as an inspiring teacher of Scripture and a most sympathetic listener to boys with personal problems. Sadly, she died only six weeks later.

The Lloyd Webber *Requiem* began to make newspaper headlines towards the end of 1984. According to the press reports, Andrew Lloyd Webber had shut himself away for four weeks in order to compose the piece. We began to realise that something big was afoot during the rehearsals of the revised version: it was announced that the *Requiem* would be recorded during Christmas choir-time, and that the world premiere would take place early the following year. The recording sessions at E.M.I.'s Abbey Road studios were an exciting feature of the pre-Christmas period. The entire choir was accommodated in the expensive *Northumberland Hotel*, overlooking Lord's cricket ground. The Choristers were thrilled to discover that their rooms were equipped with every convenience, including telephones (banned, more or less successfully), colour televisions, and in-house Swed-ish videos of doubtful suitability. An added attraction was the shoe-polishing machine – seldom have Choristers' shoes been polished with so much enthusiasm – and great joy was derived from the high-speed lifts, a delight which had to be rationed when it became evident that other guests were being marooned for long periods on the upper floors.

Andrew Lloyd Webber had made further alterations to the *Requiem* by the time we began recording. The bass soloist of the early version had been written out of the score, and the strings were replaced by the synthesiser that had so impressed the Choristers at the pilot performance. The three soloists were Sarah Brightman, Placido Domingo, and our own Paul Miles-Kingston. Time was limited and the recording sessions were gruelling, but the Choristers stood up to the pressure very well indeed. And none was more professional than the treble soloist, Paul Miles-Kingston, whose consistent, calm approach would have put many more experi-enced recording artistes to shame.

As William Clements, one of the Choristers, wrote:

One of the lessons learned was that recording sessions are not as exciting as you may think. Sometimes a session would pass without any breaks at all, but on other occasions we would have to stop and start frequently while Lorin Maazel considered various adjustments. Even so, there were moments of light relief, such as when Mr Maazel, a very relaxed conductor, let go of his baton in mid-beat, causing it to describe a perfect parabola and land at the feet of the principal 'cellist.

Inevitably, the biggest excitement was the Choir's trip to New York in February 1985 to take part in the world premiere of the *Requiem* in St Thomas's church in Fifth Avenue, together with the St Thomas's choir, the only choir in the U.S.A. to have its own choir school. Thomas Raskin takes up the tale:

After breakfast we set off to the shouts of 'Good luck' and 'Goodbye', and made our way to the west end of the Cathedral, where our coach was waiting, as were the press and television cameras: a taste of what was to come. The television company was actually going to broadcast it on our return!

From John F. Kennedy Airport we were taken by coach to the New York Hilton Hotel, and then we got down to work in St Thomas's church. The TV lights were hot, and it was very warm in the church. This was built right on top of a subway station, and in the concert a train went underneath in a very quiet bit!

On Sunday morning we went on a sight-seeing trip, which included going up the Empire State Building to the 86th floor. When we came back we went past St Thomas's church, and there were about five or six television vans outside; our guide said, 'There must be something big going on in there, though I don't know what'. We all shouted back, 'They're filming us tonight!'

The success of the *Requiem* took us all by surprise, not least the meteoric rise up the pop charts of the *Pie Jesu* movement, sung by Paul Miles-Kingston and Sarah Brightman. Soon a video version of this was filmed in Winchester Cathedral,

XXXIII (*top left*) Cathedral Choir at Niagara Falls, 26 April 1982. The party included the Bishop of Winchester, the Rt. Revd. John Taylor, and Mrs Peggy Taylor (left), and the Dean, the Very Revd. Michael Stancliffe, and Mrs Barbara Stancliffe (right)

XXXIV (*top right*) Paul Miles Kingston and golden disks awarded for the single *Pie Jesu* from the Lloyd Webber *Requiem*

XXXV (*centre*) 24 February 1985. Première of the Lloyd Webber *Requiem* in St Thomas' Church, 5th Avenue, New York. Placido Domingo, Sarah Brightman, Paul Miles Kingston, Andrew Lloyd Webber, Lorin Maazel

XXXVI (*bottom left*) Quiristers and Choristers in Vienna, 2 March 1986, for a performance of the Lloyd Webber *Requiem* at the *Konzerthaus* which was filled with smoke for the purpose. It was nevertheless a thrill to be associated with a musical event that had so established itself in public consciousness: Paul was nearly mobbed by a group of pubescent girls during a choir-time outing, and on another occasion we stopped to refuel the school mini-bus only to hear the *Pie Jesu* blaring from a nearby loudspeaker.

Whatever the artistic merits of the *Requiem*, it served one important function: the general public was made more aware of the existence of cathedral choirs. The venture no doubt played its part in boosting the number of applicants at the annual voice trials, at a time when other cathedral and collegiate choirs were struggling to recruit young singers.

The year 1985 was a record one for music scholarships: no fewer than eight boys were successful at various schools. We were visited by the Bishop of Winchester, the Right Revd. John Taylor, who bade us farewell on his retirement. He was succeeded by the Right Revd. Colin James, Bishop of Wakefield, a former Bishop of Basingstoke and Pilgrims' parent, and no stranger to the Close. The busy Easter term ended with perfomances of *The Master of Dotheboys Hall*, a dramatised version of Dickens's *Nicholas Nickleby*, written and produced by Jeremy Edwards.

The Choristers' Easter holiday was interrupted when the Cathedral Choir gave the British premiere of the Lloyd Webber *Requiem* in Westminster Abbey. This was conceived as a memorial to those who had died in the I.R.A.'s bomb attack during the Conservative Party Conference at Brighton the previous November. Amongst those killed had been a Pilgrims' parent, Mrs. Wakeham. In the congregation were many prominent members of the Government, including the Prime Minister, and they were evidently moved by music which, as the composer explained in a programme note, had been inspired by similar atrocities. After the recital members of the Choir attended a reception at No.12 Downing Street, kindly given by the Government Chief Whip, the Rt. Hon. John Wakeham. Shortly before the Winchester party was due to leave, Mrs. Thatcher arrived and took the Choristers on a tour of the building. We were soon astonished to find ourselves in the front hall of No.10. To prove the point, the Prime Minister opened the familiar black door, to the consternation of the policeman on duty outside.

A month or two later Paul Miles-Kingston's professional engagements continued with a visit to Wembley Stadium, where he watched the Cup Final in the company of Placido Domingo. By that time *Pie Jesu* had reached No.3 in the pop charts, a position which it held for a fortnight.

At morning Assembly on 6 June, Mr. Kefford announced that Humphrey Salwey had died peacefully during the night. It was typical of Humphrey's continuing interest in the development of the school that had been his life that only a few days previously he had been seen in College Street quietly copying down the Winchester College Election results. No less profound was his love of the Cathedral which he had served for so many years, and the day before he died he had been actively involved in his daily task of counting the offerings made by visitors in the collecting boxes. Humphrey's funeral, on Friday 14 July 1985, was attended by many Old Pilgrims, present boys and members of staff. The Choristers and Quiristers combined to sing 'How Lovely are thy Dwellings Fair' from Brahms' *German Requiem* and Walford Davies' anthem *God Be in my Head*, which had closed so many school concerts years ago.

The Dean of Winchester gave the Address:

We have come together to support Humphrey, Lorna and their children with our presence, our prayers and our praises. I do in fact believe that, in ways I do not profess to understand, our presence and our prayers may be of some help to Humphrey also – who must be feeling, where he is now, just a bit of the loneliness and bewilderment of the New Boy!

We give praises to God for all He has given through Humphrey to so many for 85 years: Humphrey the child of the parsonage; the Westminster schoolboy; the 18-year-old officer in the Grenadier Guards; the undergraduate at Christ Church; the athlete and the mountaineer; the founder, with Dean Selwyn, of The Pilgrims' School, and its Headmaster for 32 years; the Winchester magistrate; the member of the Cathedral Foundation for 54 years; the husband of Lorna for 60 years less eight weeks and three days.

But it is not so much the length as the quality of his service that is remarkable. As schoolmaster, as citizen and as churchman he has consistently given a shining example of qualities that are very precious today: humility, self-discipline, loyalty, truthfulness, straightness and sheer integrity – all of which made him of so great worth that he has been a trusted, respected and greatly beloved father to so very many whom he included in his family.

As founder of THE Pilgrims' School, Humphrey was THE Pilgrim *par excellence*. For the chief quality required of a Pilgrim is valour: 'Who would true valour see, Let him come hither.' Valour is courage, and Humphrey had great courage; but it is very much more than that. It is 'value', 'worth' – it is the sum of all those worthy, worthwhile qualities mentioned earlier.

After the service a slow procession followed the coffin out of the Cathedral, including the Head Commoner, Edward Harris, carrying the staff that Humphrey, as High Steward of the Cathedral, had himself borne in procession for so many years.

With the death of Humphrey Salwey we all felt that an era in the life of the school had ended, and this impression was reinforced at the end of the summer term, when two long-serving members of the staff moved from Winchester. First, Dick and Islay Kitson retired to the home that they had bought in Scotland. During 27 years at The Pilgrims' Dick had served under five headmasters. One of them, Martin Briggs, wrote a tribute to his Deputy Headmaster for *The Pilgrims' School Magazine*:

Throughout his career Dick has set himself high standards, and others, seeing this, have striven to live up to them: in teaching and learning, on the games field, in personal standards of behaviour – no-one has ever liked to feel that they have let Dick down. He set us all an example in the rock-like reliability of everything he did, his grasp of detail, and in his unfailing courtesy to everyone.

To the younger boys (some of whom genuinely thought that the portrait in the front hall was not of Dean Selwyn but of Dick!) he may have initially seemed a remote and austere figure, but not for long. They came to recognise

XXXVII (*top left*) Dick Kitson and Colin Thompson, Athletics Finals, 1985

XXXVIII (*top right*) Michael Kefford and fundraisers for the Listen for Life appeal, a charity set up by Nigel and Liz Kinloch to provide monitoring devices to prevent cot deaths. December 1987

XXXIX (*centre*) Richard and Maureen Jackson and the Quiristers, in Winchester College cloisters, 1987

XL (*bottom right*) July 1988. Members of the 1st XI (Francis Brett, Piers Cardiff, James Urquhart, William Sawrey Cookson (Captain)) meet Mike Gatting at Finchley Cricket Club

him as a kind and sympathetic judge of their character who knew when to encourage and when to administer a rocket, and taught them Classics with painstaking skill. They knew that he had their interests at the heart of everything he did.

At the same time, Colin and Lesley Thompson moved to Cothill House School, Abingdon. Colin had acted as teacher and mentor to many generations of Pilgrims' boys. He was an enthusiastic Set Master of the Wrens and, together with Lesley, had looked after Quiristers' School for two years. Above all, together with Keith Ross, he had been responsible for master-minding the whole games scene, and raising the standard of Pilgrims' sports to new heights.

So when school resumed in the middle of September 1985 there were new faces to welcome on the staff: Colin Webster arrived to teach Classics, and Richard Jackson returned to England from a spell in Kenya to teach History (in eventual succession to Ambrose Streatfeild as Head of Department) and, with his wife Maureen, to take over the running of Quiristers' School and maintain the unique family atmosphere of that distant colony of the Pilgrims' empire. Finally, if a school, like an army, marches on its stomach, then we were particularly fortunate to secure the services of Gardner Merchant's 'Catering Manager of the Year', Miss Gill Jones.

For the Choristers the academic year 1985–6 could be called 'The Year of the Foreign Tours'. During the Christmas Half-Term there came a goodwill visit to Fleury-sur-Loire. Ever since the 900th anniversary celebrations, Winchester Cathedral – a former Benedictine monastery – had been twinned with the Benedictine community of Fleury thanks to Dean Michael Stancliffe, and a visit to Fleury was long overdue. We were warmly welcomed by the mònks. The male members of the party, plus Mary Taylor, were accommodated in the priory guest-house, and the Lay Clerks and boys ate with the monks in the impressive quietness of their refectory. Young Pilgrims are used to being put on silence at meal-times, but the Choristers' astonishment on learning that the whole community ate in silence was a joy to behold. The high point of the trip was when we joined the monks in prayer: at the solemn vespers of their Foundation, and at High Mass on the Sunday morning. We came away from Fleury spiritually uplifted, and not a little humbled.

The second trip was to Vienna, where the Choristers joined forces in a televised concert with the Vienna Boys' Choir, the Petits Chanteurs de Paris, and the Tölzer Knabenchor. Naturally much of the boys' time was taken up with rehearsals, but a few hours were made free, and the British Council representative had kindly organised a tour of Vienna and its environs. So we drove out to Kloster Neuburg, visited one of Beethoven's houses, and returned to the city via the Vienna Woods, where the first winter snow was lying thick.

Then on 1 March 1986 John Crook and Mary Taylor were astonished to find themselves once again in Vienna, together with Richard Jackson, Elizabeth Kefford, 35 Choristers and Quiristers and an augmented team of Lay Clerks. The purpose of the visit was to perform Andrew Lloyd Webber's *Requiem* at the Konzerthaus, in a performance conducted by Lorin Maazel. Richard Kaye rejoined the Choir for the weekend and sang the treble solo. This was the first time that Choristers and Quiristers had sung together in a major musical event;

it proved to be a remarkably happy partnership, which more recently has been continued in a series of recordings for Decca with Christopher Hogwood.

Finally, the Cathedral Choir went on tour in the United States for nearly three weeks after Easter. Our first port of call was Dallas, where we visited Southfork Ranch, home of the long-running American 'soap'. Thereafter the Choir followed a curious course around the North American continent: the Deep Southern town of Macon (Georgia), notable for its Indian burial mounds; New York, where we sang at the Alice Tully Hall; Toronto, where the recital was given in the Roy Thompson Hall; Minneapolis; Denver; San Francisco; Los Angeles; and Boston. Rehearsal time was kept to a minimum by the provision of two programmes, 'A' and 'B', which alternated at each venue. Highlights of the tour included a ride on the cable-cars of San Francisco and a visit to Disneyland. Much music was performed and an incredible mileage covered by air.

For the Quiristers, there were moments of musical excitement nearer home during this extraordinary year, notably an invitation for six of them to sing at Leeds Castle at Edward Heath's 70th birthday party. A choir of 13 singers performed madrigals, and the traditional Winchester College Graces were sung to the illustrious company, which read very much like a 'Who's Who' of Conservative politicians past and present.

Not to be outdone, many of the Commoners were involved in two memorable school plays. In December 1985 Clement McWilliam produced and conducted a musical version of the biblical story *Tobias and the Angel*, and the following term Jeremy Edwards wrote for the Juniors a dramatised version of Roald Dahl's *James and the Giant Peach*. This was an outstanding production, for which Marjory Monro designed some marvellous costumes, particularly those of eight boys playing the outsized bugs whose home was a magic peach.

At the end of the school year there were some important farewells to be made. Dean Stancliffe had recently suffered from a serious illness, and took his retirement in September, after 16 years in Winchester. Michael and Barbara Stancliffe retired to Pickering in North Yorkshire. Sadly, Michael did not enjoy a lengthy retirement but died early the following year. His body was brought back to the Cathedral he had served so well, and was buried in the cloister garth. Appropriately, Bishop John Taylor preached the sermon at his Requiem Mass, on 11 April 1987:

Michael Stancliffe conveyed to others his conviction that this is a place where prayer has been valid (to quote from his favourite T.S. Eliot) and can be valid still. He knew himself to be the curator of that living Benedictine stream of ordered worship which has given these stones their *raison d'être* for more than nine centuries, and for him it was no gesture of modern ecumenism to revive the link with the Brothers of Saint Benoît-sur-Loire.

The steady unobtrusive reiteration day by day of the Offices and pre-eminently of the Eucharist was, he believed, like the ancient springs that flow beneath the Cathedral, the source from which the very stones derive their undeniable power of stopping casual tourists in their tracks and opening their eyes in sudden recognition to see a door opened in heaven.

The summer term 1986 also saw the retirement of Ambrose Streatfeild, of whom

XLI 5 December 1986. The coachi
song, concluding *Let's Make an Ope*
The cast includes (left to right) Al
Mottram and Kenneth Tewkesbur

XLII 13 March 1987. A scene from
Scapino Sorts it out. Jonathan
Kennedy (Hyacintha), William
Nevin (Scapino), Jasper Chalcraft
(Silvester), Francis Bartholomew
(Zerbinetta)

XLIII 10 June 1987. Pilgrims' Schoo
boys join Winchester College to form
the cast of the National Youth Musi
Theatre in *Salomon Pavey* at the Theat
Royal Winchester

Michael Kefford wrote, 'When I first came, he gave me the impression he was permanently on duty, as it was impossible to cross the yard, attend a meal, an assembly, a school service, or other occasion, without finding Ambrose actively employed, helping boys, being interested in their various problems or successes at school or at home, or merely taking a very active part in the events of the moment. The highly professional airman had surely found his true vocation when he laid aside his wings and became a teacher.'

At the same time John Crook retired from full-time schoolmastering and continued to care for the Choristers and edit the school *Magazine*, and Jeremy Edwards moved to a day-school in London.

As a result of these departures the autumn term of 1986 saw many new faces in the Close. During the summer holidays it had been announced that Dean Stancliffe's successor would be Canon Trevor Beeson, of St Margaret's, Westminster. He was formally installed on 7 February 1987, and shortly afterwards paid the school the first of many visits, coming to morning Assembly. Other new members of staff included Andy Perry and Jonathan Thomson-Glover, no stranger to The Pilgrims' as he had helped us out for a term during the 1981 Jubilee celebrations.

Once again, the school year started with a sponsored walk, masterminded by Keith Ross, which raised £4,576 for the Hampshire County Hospital Body Scanner Appeal. Our route took us along the Itchen Navigation Canal, up Plague Pits Valley, over the golf course to Morestead and up the long path to Cheesefoot Head. At this point the juniors stopped for a weary picnic lunch, while the senior boys put in an extra four miles by walking nearly to Ovington Down Farm and back. For the adults, the walk was tinged by sadness that this could be the last time we trod this particular route, threatened as it was by the proposed M3 Motorway extension: we were not to know how long the resolution of that thorny issue was to take!

One more farewell had to be made before 1986 was out: to Clement McWilliam. Ambrose Streatfeild resumed his career at the next O.P. Day, laying particular emphasis on Clement's physical and intellectual energy and expressing the admiration we have all felt at the way Clement transformed The Pilgrims' School into the most musical preparatory school in the country.

If 1985–6 was The Year of the Choir Tour, then 1986–7 was The Year of the Play. Pilgrims' boys – mostly Commoners – were involved in three widely contrasting productions. In his final fortnight at The Pilgrims' School Clement McWilliam produced, yet again, *Let's Make an Opera*. The following term the Pilgrims' Hall was magically transformed into a Venetian piazza, when Colin Webster staged an English version of one of Molière's lesser-known plays, *Les Fourberies de Scapin*. Music for the entr'actes from Stravinsky *Pulcinella* suite was provided by an all-boy orchestra conducted by Hilary Brooks. William Nevin, as Scapino, had the major rôle in the play, and his inspired acting brought out the best in those who played opposite him.

Finally, a large contingent of Pilgrims' boys, whose talents in the previous productions had been recognised, was recruited to join boys from Winchester College in *The Ballad of Salomon Pavey* by Jeremy James Taylor and David Drew-Smythe. This was staged by the National Youth Music Theatre, first at the

Theatre Royal, Winchester, and subsequently at the Edinburgh Festival. The play was based on the life of choristers at the Chapel Royal, Windsor, and was inspired by Ben Jonson's *Epitaph on S.P., a child of the Chapel Royal*, whose subject, Jonson tells us, was celebrated for his portrayal of old men but died at the age of thirteen. Pilgrims' boys took the part of Chapel Royal and St Paul's choristers as this poignant story unfurled.

As impressive as these dramatic productions was the continued improvement in the school's musical standards, now in the capable hands of Hilary Brooks, Head of Music, together with Michael Wood, one of whose first actions on joining the staff was to form a band. At the Summer Concert this new ensemble gave a stylish performance of the *Promenade* from Mussorgsky's *Pictures at an Exhibition*.

In 1987 came the departure of three other members of staff who had set their own personal stamp on the life of the school. Stuart Roberts retired after 10 years of mathematics teaching. During that time he had run the Saxons' Set with enthusiasm (many Old Pilgrims recall with pleasure the secret meetings at which 'Saxons' Snaxons' were consumed), founded a successful model club, introduced the school to a completly new subject – computing – and created a new school team in each major sport, the Foals. He took retirement in March – four months earlier than he had foreseen – in order to care for his wife, Josanne, who was terminally ill.

In July John Baker left the Pilgrims' fold eventually to join another community a mile or so south of the Cathedral Close: the Brethren of St Cross. He had come to the school as a teacher of Geography after a career in broadcasting, and his technical ability proved invaluable. Printing especially was an activity in which the non-academic boy could excel, and the Geography Room became a common room for various crafts and activities which John encouraged as a voluntary, unofficial part of the curriculum. Above all, many generations of Pilgrims' boys have reason to be grateful to him for his patient and conscientious teaching. At the same time we bade farewell to Marian Tewkesbury, who had taken over the teaching of Scripture from Jane Stear, and as well as increasing the boys' knowledge of Bible stories had given them a profound insight into many other religious matters – as well as being a sensitive counsellor.

Our sadness at the departure of these long-serving members of staff was tempered by excitement at the thought of new challenges that lay ahead. For 1987 was very much a turning point in the history of the school, as plans were made for a major addition to the premises. As we consider the history of the school, it becomes apparent that its continued success is intimately bound up with its physical fabric. Successive headmasters of The Pilgrims' School have set their stamp on the school as much in terms of the additions that they have added to its premises as in the staff they have appointed and the changes they have made to the day-to-day running of the establishment. Not for nothing did Humphrey Salwey lay particular emphasis in his first editorial in *The Pilgrims' School Magazine* on the beauty of the surroundings: the words he wrote for the school's first prospectus are still used almost unaltered today:

The whole setting of the school, among the ancient buildings of the Cathedral, the College and Wolvesey, is a living source of inspiration as well as an ever-present reminder of history and tradition.

As founding Headmaster, he was responsible, with Dean Selwyn's encouragement, for turning a rambling canonry house into an efficient preparatory school; for the adaptation to educational purposes of two historic buildings, the Pilgrims' Hall and the Priory Stabling; and, at the very end of his long tenure of office, for the reconstruction of the buildings on the south side of the yard to form the teaching block subsequently named after him. Rodney Blake's tenure of office saw the acquisition of New Piece and accommodation in Wellington House, and the construction of a tennis court. The 'Selwyn Building' was completed thanks to an appeal masterminded by his successor, Martin Briggs. The school premises grew again during Stephen McWatters' headmastership, with the construction of the new music practice room (identified many years previously as a pressing need) and the extension of the changing room and domestic facilities.

But these additions were not enough, and soon after his arrival, and with the full backing of the Governing Body, Michael Kefford conceived the idea of a radical enlargement of the school buildings. Plans were produced, and in September 1987 a Pilgrims' School Appeal was launched with a formal supper in the Pilgrims' Hall for the Appeal Committee and members of staff; the cream of Pilgrims' instrumentalists provided music. A professional Appeal Director, Mr. Bernard Ashford, was appointed and lived in the school, and a tiny office was provided for him in the attic above the Deputy Headmaster's flat.

Amidst all the excitement of the Appeal, no less momentous things were happening in the Cathedral. At 11.30 a.m. on Monday 13 July 1987, the news broke: Martin Neary had been appointed Organist and Master of the Choristers at Westminster Abbey from 1 January 1988. Appropriately – though by sheer coincidence – his last Southern Cathedrals Festival was at Winchester. The following term was musically as busy as ever, with a prestigious performance of Duruflé's *Requiem* in the Royal Festival Hall, in which the 'cello solo was admirably played by Alice Neary. But farewell parties for Martin became more and more frequent as Christmas approached, culminating in a dinner at *The Wykeham Arms* organised by the Lay Clerks.

By then, we knew that Martin's successor would be Mr. David Hill, Organist of Westminster Cathedral. There was a term's interregnum before Mr. Hill's arrival, during which the running of the Cathedral's music was placed in the capable hands of the Sub-Organist, Timothy Byram-Wigfield. David Hill was installed at Evensong on Sunday 1 May 1988, and he and his wife Hilary soon became familiar figures in the Cathedral Close. Hilary Hill began to take over the training of the Choristers' voices.

For many years this task had been undertaken by Kenneth Tewkesbury, who left the staff in July after 21 years. He had contributed in many fields: in the classroom as history teacher and form-master of C1, and in the Cathedral as a tenor Lay Clerk. His performances in three productions of *The Little Sweep* will long be remembered. He and Marian moved to the West Country, where Ken quickly attracted singing pupils.

Meanwhile the red thermometer indicating the progress of the Appeal continued to rise, and a team from the City Archaeologist's office dug the trial trenches required by English Heritage, without discovering anything of major historical significance. When the boys returned for the summer term, 1988, they discovered that the Quiet Room (that prefabricated haven of peace where the drum kit was formerly practised) had been razed to the ground to make way for the new building, and for the next five weeks the school echoed to a different rhythm: the thud of the pile-driver as 35 steel tubes were hammered into the ground.

A major event for the Quirister during that summer term was Winchester College's production of *Carmen* in New Hall. The choice of this opera caused a raised eyebrow or two when its reviewer mentioned the fact outside Winchester circles. A tale of sexual infatuation in southern Spain on a public school stage? How would even Wykeham's great foundation provide soloists with the stamina to cope with the demanding major rôles? Producer Jo Bain overcame the casting problems by the judicious use of four professional soloists, and the cast was further augmented by girls from St Swithun's School (no small boys lopsidedly bolstered with cushions in this production), while mothers, wives and other figures well known to us swelled the chorus of cigarette girls, gypsies and passers-by. Most prominent of all in the crowd scenes were the urchins played by our own Quiristers, all of whom displayed enviable acting talent.

Not that dramatic ability had been absent from our own community during the year. In September 1987 Robin Perry, soon known to boys and staff alike as 'Pez', to distinguish him from his namesake Andrew Perry, had joined us as English teacher and master in charge of drama. At the end of his first term he had staged Alan Ayckbourn's comedy *Ernie's Incredible Illucinations* (sic), for which the Quiristers again provided a musical framework, accompanied by Richard Jackson on his guitar. Not to be outdone, Colin Webster produced *The Government Inspector*, in an innovative transposition of Gogol's 1836 play to a British West Indian island. Marvellous music directed by Michael Wood (Head Quirister, Tom Seligman, learned to play the steel drums for the occasion), superb costumes provided, yet again, by Marjory Monro, and a colourful set designed by Jonathan Thomson-Glover, made this a play to be long remembered and provided acting opportunities for a cast of 54, including the 'screaming brats' from the J Block.

No account of Pilgrims' School drama would be complete without mention of the annual J-Block Nativity celebrations, skilfully and sensitively produced each December by Ann Coggan and Margaret Humphrys, and performed before an invited audience of parents and friends in the Pilgrims' Hall. For many, it is the high spot of the school's Christmas calendar.

The new importance accorded to drama was just one of several changes made to the curriculum during the late 1980s. In Geography, a new emphasis was laid on practical field work, and Bob Wood, who had joined the staff in April 1987, brought his own teaching skill and enthusiasm to this aspect of the subject. In the first year groups of boys were driven out to King's Worthy or to the Badger Farm estate, where they interviewed the startled populace on their shopping habits, before analysing the results. Accounts of Mr. Wood's other geographical outings appeared in the *Magazine*: a farm visit for members of B Block, and an investigation of flow dynamics in the River Meon. In one experiment dog biscuits (being non-polluting and fun for the fish), were used to measure the velocity of the water in various parts of the river.

At around the same time the Art Department achieved the standing it deserved, when it became a fully time-tabled part of the curriculum rather than an alternative to afternoon sport. The work produced in the Art Room under Marjory Monro's inspired guidance reached even greater heights, as was apparent from the splendid displays mounted in the dining room; more and more boys urged to be allowed to use the Art Room in their spare time, and the number of Art scholarships and bursaries increased.

Under Margot Meredith's direction, Pilgrims' boys had long excelled in Science, and the school had been one of the first to use the Nuffield Science Project. The subject grew in stature and a second science teacher, Richard Kimberley, was appointed in 1988, eventually replacing Margot as Head of Science on her retirement. Computing was elevated to the status of a full-time subject at the same time, and class music assumed a new importance: within a few years every form in the school enjoyed a double period of class music each week. The school's own full-time teacher of P.E., Chris Rose, was appointed in September 1988. As a result of all these changes, the average age of the staff was as young as it had ever been, and the calibre of the teaching personnel was evident from increasingly fine results in scholarships, Common Entrance and the Winchester Entrance examination.

A sad event during the year was the closure of West Downs, with whom we had enjoyed such friendly rivalry on the games field for many years. Several boys transferred from West Downs to The Pilgrims' and one master, Kenneth Lay, joined us as a teacher of Mathematics. It was fitting that the Headmaster of West Downs, Mr. Jerry Cornes, was our guest at Prize Giving two years later, when the last of his former pupils left The Pilgrims' after very successful careers here.

By the start of the autumn term 1988 the 'new building' was approaching completion. In place of the stacks of bricks and a few low walls that we had left in July we found a full-height building, complete with roof (as yet untiled) and an elegant colonnade on the garden side. Suddenly it no longer seemed impossible that we should move in by Christmas. And the building had a name: it was decided that it should be called after the late Dean, Michael Stancliffe. Thus the 'Stancliffe Building' joined the 'Salwey Building' and the 'Selwyn Building' as a memorial to a Dean who had shown a benevolent interest in the school, and particularly in the choir.

The Christmas term was enlivened by another sponsored walk, which brought in the sum of £5,568, shared between the Great Ormond Street Children's Hospital and our own Appeal. A further £5,396 was raised by a Gala Concert on a wet and stormy night early in October, when the combined Choristers and Quiristers joined international celebrities in an exciting programme of songs, instrumental solos, duets and ensembles. Humphrey Burton introduced the music and the performers included Peter Frankl and Barry Tuckwell. All three joined together for an encore – six hands on one piano. For the reviewer the most satisfying music was provided by the Purcell songs in the second half of the programme, 'exquisite miniatures, performed with subtlety and conviction by Charles Brett, supported by the discreet accompaniment of Timothy Byram-Wigfield on the harpsichord and Hilary Brooks on the baroque 'cello'. Other fund-raising events included a fashion show of second-hand clothes organised by a parent, Angela Cardiff. The six models included the Headmaster's daughter, Alison Kefford, and the twin sisters of a current Pilgrim.

At the end of the Christmas term a steady stream of boy helpers carried books and furniture from various classrooms to the new building, which was virtually complete. The finishing touches were put to the outside of the building during the holidays; a combination of exceptionally mild weather and the Bursar's skill in persuading the builders to forego their normal Christmas break brought about a magical transformation of the garden area. With astonishing speed the desolate waste of the site surrounding the new building was landscaped and turfed over, garden features were created, including a pond, and paths were laid linking various parts of the teaching complex. At the same time the dining room was enlarged by moving the end wall eight feet further south, and a boys' common room area was created from the former senior and junior classrooms.

The design of the new building was carefully conceived to incorporate elements of the existing school buildings: the profile of its hipped roof, for example, recalled that of the Pilgrims' Hall, and timber studding at first-floor level echoed the timber-framing of the Priory Stabling Block. The main façade faced south over the garden: two projecting wings, containing music practice rooms and the stairwell, framed a colonnade supporting a gallery. On the ground floor were a large hall, music practice rooms, and the new English Room; at first floor level were classrooms for Geography, History and French. The former French Room in the Selwyn building was now given over to Science, doubling the space available to that subject.

In this way all teaching was moved out of the school buildings of 1932–3. The school retained, however, the use of Wellington House, where Ann Coggan and Margaret Humphrys continued their patient work in sowing the seeds of academic success further up the school. Prospective parents of junior boys are always taken 'over the road' to Wellington House and are invariably impressed with the quality of work done in 'JA' and 'JM'; and rightly so – for here the foundations are laid on which others will build. The Pilgrims' School has been fortunate indeed in its succession of junior form teachers.

Gala Concert apart, the year 1988–9 was a golden year for music and drama at The Pilgrims' School. Robin Perry wrote a play for the Christmas term: *Macbeth plc*, an updated version of Shakespeare's tragedy in which Duncan was Chairman of 'Scotcorp', Macbeth was a stockbroker with ambition, and the witches were represented by HAL, a computer. The music for the play was written and conducted by the Head Quirister, Tom Seligman; a first-rate achievement. In the Easter term Hilary Brooks produced (and conducted) Richard Rodney Bennett's 'opera for young people', *All the King's Men*; the second time this work has been performed at The Pilgrims'. Drama even found its way into school assemblies, when Andrew Perry encouraged playlets to illustrate the theme of daily worship. Andy was an inspiring young teacher of Scripture, who left us all too soon for a career in the Church. However, the school was extraordinarily lucky in recruiting an equally talented replacement, Andrew Moore, who carried on The Pilgrims' tradition of caring concern and inspirational Scripture teaching.

Musical events included informal concerts, a special recital by prospective music scholars, and a summer concert of the high standard we have come to

XLIV 28 April 1989. HRH The Princess Margaret opens the Stancliffe Building. Julian Smith conducts the combined Choristers and Quiristers in Schubert's setting of the 23rd Psalm.

XLV Princess Margaret tours the school with the Dean, Michael Kefford and Bursar David Feast

XLVI The youngest boy in the school, Billy Tibbits, presents a bouquet to Princess Margaret

XLVII The Stancliffe Building in 1991, when the Cathedral tower was scaffolded for repairs

expect of Pilgrims' musicians, thanks to the dedicated work of Hilary Brooks, Michael Wood and their assistants. Quirister Mark Hollings was much in demand, and appeared at the Aldeburgh festival in the part of the Angel in Britten's *The Burning Fiery Furnace*. Four of the Quiristers spent three days in Madrid in May 1989 recording Beethoven's *Ode to Joy* in connection with the European parliamentary elections.

The greatest excitement of the year was the opening of the 'Stancliffe Building' by Her Royal Highness The Princess Margaret, on Friday 28 April 1989. The weather, which had been disappointingly cold throughout the earlier part of the week, suddenly showed a miraculous improvement, and we enjoyed temperatures more appropriate to July. After lunch, parents and boys began to assemble on the lawn in front of the Stancliffe Building, and Her Royal Highness arrived shortly before two o'clock, having landed by helicopter at Bar End. At the front door she was greeted by the Lord Lieutenant of Hampshire, the Dean, and the Mayor of Winchester, and permission was sought to present to the Princess the Headmaster and Governors of the school.

The Service of Inauguration opened with the singing of The Pilgrims' hymn *He who Would Valiant Be*, and the Head Commoner, Ian van Every, read from I Corinthians 3, vv. 9–17: 'For other foundation can no man lay than that is laid, which is Jesus Christ'. The Dean led prayers, after which the combined Commoners' Choirs sang Roger Quilter's setting of Rudyard Kipling's poem *Non Nobis, Domine*, accompanied by the Orchestra. Then the Stancliffe Building was dedicated by the Bishop of Winchester. After the singing of the hymn *All People that on Earth do Dwell* Her Royal Highness unveiled a commemorative plaque and declared the Stancliffe Building open. Billy Tibbits, the youngest boy in the school, presented her with a bouquet. Then the crowds made their way to a marquee in Mirabel Close for tea, while the Headmaster and Governors accompanied the Princess on a tour of inspection of the new building. In the evening those few boys whose parents were unable to take them out enjoyed a barbeque on the lawn, then all made their way to Wolvesey Palace, where the castle ruins formed a splendid back-drop to a magnificent firework display.

After such excitements, the remainder of the summer term might have seemed rather tame. But normal school life quickly resumed (if life at The Pilgrims' School can ever be described as normal!). At the end of the year we bade farewell to Margot Meredith, who for 20 years had brilliantly taught Science to generations of Pilgrims, and to Andy Perry; they were replaced by Judith Whiticar and Andy Moore respectively.

The range of activities available to Pilgrims' boys was increased thanks to the enthusiasm of Allan Mottram, who took parties of boys to Brittany each Easter, and Colin Webster, Jonathan Thomson-Glover and Robin Perry, who continued the tradition of school ski trips and introduced summer adventure weeks in the Brecon mountains. Jonathan Thomson-Glover communicated his love of tennis, wind-surfing and fly-fishing to several generations of boys, and was greatly missed when he took a new post at Clifton College in July 1990; fortunately a Pilgrims' parent, Gillian Hamilton, was on hand to take on his skilful work in the French Department.

Early in October 1989 the Cathedral Choir experienced, once again, the excitement of foreign travel, with a mini-tour to Paris, to take part in a concert with the European Baroque Chamber Orchestra in the church of Saint-Eustache – part of a *Festival d'Art Sacré* organised by the City of Paris. The conductor on this occasion was the father of one of the Choristers, Roy Goodman.

A month later, an era in the life of The Pilgrims' School was finally closed, with the death of Lorna Salwey at the age of 90. At her funeral on 2 November, Desmond Farley, one of the 'aboriginals' who had transferred from the old Choir School to The Pilgrims' in September 1931, recalled with affection the caring concern exercised by Lorna during the first 32 years of the school's existence, and her continuing interest in Pilgrims past and present.

As the Choristers returned from the Cathedral in solemn silence, the hearse drove slowly past the building that Lorna loved so well: the Pilgrims' Hall that had given the school its name; the 17th-century house where Humphrey and Lorna had lived for 32 years; the Priory Stabling Block that they had so proudly acquired to expand the school premises. Then the long, black car turned through the arch and was lost from view. It was a poignant moment.

With the 1990s came the new demands of the National Curriculum. At the start of the Christmas term 1990 the staff returned to school a day early, in order to discuss ways in which their various subjects could be co-ordinated. The physical expression of the new syllabus was the modernisation of the old carpentry shop, scarcely altered since the 1950s, into a new technology centre, and a teacher of technology, Mr. Hilditch, joined the staff. By quite small modifications to the daily routine, Keith Ross cunningly managed to fit in an extra lesson on Monday and Friday afternoons. New subjects appeared on the timetable: Information Technology, Technology, Expressive Arts. The range of activities available to boys during 'Commoners' was expanded, with the introduction of Current Affairs, and encouragement was given to modelling.

And so we have come to The Pilgrims' 60th year. It is interesting to enquire why the school has survived, whereas so many preparatory schools – even, alas, West Downs, our ancient rival – have been forced into reluctant oblivion. Where are the hundred schools of Eastbourne and Seaford? And why do parents incur future bills of nearly £4,000 *per annum* by adding their sons' names to the keenly-competed entrance list, usually when those sons are too young to be asked their views on the matter?

As far as the survival of the school is concerned, no doubt its physical situation has played an important part. Flanked by the Cathedral on the one hand, and Winchester College on the other, The Pilgrims' School, though financially independent of both, can count on the support of the two ancient foundations, and benefit from the expertise of their representatives on the Governing Body and Advisory Council. Unlike the luckless dinosaur, The Pilgrims' School has developed its own secret of survival: a happy ability to adapt to changing situations. Throughout the past 50 years it has provided a kind of education entirely appropriate to the times.

As to the second question, the situation of the school must surely influence parents in their choice of school: it would be hard to imagine a more agreeable site than our corner of the Cathedral Close. More important still are the people to whom those parents entrust their sons for education. The staff of The Pilgrims' School is as diverse as any in its range of skills, interests, previous experience, and temperament. The common factor seems to be a sense of intense personal involvement in the life of the school and the boys it educates, not at some abstract level, but in the down-to-earth business of shared experience – educational, artistic, sporting. Visitors to the school are struck by the close rapport between staff and boys: something of Spencer Leeson's 'large family' ideal has survived, even in an establishment of over 200 staff and boys. The boarders are especially privileged to be cared for by such a devoted team of matrons. Nor should the outstanding devotion of many long-term members of the school's domestic staff be overlooked.

Equally important is the increasing involvement of the parents in the life of The Pilgrims' School, not merely as customers seeking value for money in the education of their children but, as we have seen, as active contributors to the life of the foundation. In recent years, increasing numbers of boys have joined the school whose fathers are themselves Old Pilgrims, forging new links with the past.

Perhaps the boys should have the last word. What do Old Pilgrims remember when they reflect on those influential days spent within the Cathedral Close? Firstly, perhaps, they remember the buildings, with their wealth of historical association. Throughout these pages we have tried to emphasise the influence that the buildings of the Cathedral Close must surely have on those who work here. Some will undoubtedly cherish vivid memories of keenly-contested matches on the games field: the heroic tussle of The Pilgrims' David against Horris Hill's Goliath, perhaps, or some individual success in an Inter-Set Match. For others, there will be the indelible recollection of performing in an orchestra playing 'real' music – a symphonic fragment, perhaps – or their first experience of acting on the tiny Pilgrims' Hall stage. But, most importantly of all, they will remember the staff. Scarcely a week passes without an Old Pilgrim casually dropping in to enquire with genuine interest after some adult member of the school who exercised a particular influence during that boy's time here in the Close. The Pilgrims' staff must be second to none in its range of expertise and in its caring commitment to the boys in its care. Lucky Pilgrims' boys to have been prepared in such a community for their journey through life.

Return of the Pilgrim

How small the Yard has grown, where once did I
Defend with bat my wicket on the wall.
Ah, 'In or Over!', that familiar call,
As swifts around the Priory steeply fly.
Those new-mown fields of contest, Castle by,
Those ancient, song-drenched rafters in the Hall,
The great Cathedral watching over all.
Flood back the memories with a sigh . . .
No need to yearn for that totality
Of youthful years, from wordly worry free!
There is no absolute reality
Save God; so what my childish eyes did see
Will tinge my vision till finality.
These things were mine; mine they will always be.

Stuart Roberts

SOURCES AND CROSS-REFERENCES

Notes to Chapter One

1. A. W. Goodman, 'The Ancestry of the Pilgrims' School', *Pilgrims' School Magazine* Vol. I no.10 (1941), p.9ff.

2. A. F. Leach, *A History of Winchester College*, London (1899), p.26ff.

3. Thos. Symonds (ed.), *Regularis Concordia*, Nelson, London (1953), p.26

4. quoted by R. N. Quirk, 'The Saxon Cathedral', *Winchester Cathedral Record* 25 (1956), p.12ff.

5. Walter Howard Frere (ed.), *The Winchester Troper*, London (1894)

6. Cecil Deedes (ed.), *Registrum Johannis de Pontissara*, London (1915), Vol. I, p.128

7. G. W. Kitchin (ed.), *Obedientiary Rolls of St Swithun*, Hants Record Soc., London (1892), p.280

8. *Register of William Waynflete, Bishop*, MS Hants Record Office, Vol. II, folio 75v

9. G. W. Kitchin, op. cit., p.398

10. Joan Greatrex (ed.), *Register of the Common Seal, I*, Winchester (1978), p.19

11. G. W. Kitchin, op. cit., p.443 (Roll of John Eode, Almoner, 1438)

12. W. H. B. Bird (ed.), *The Black Book of Winchester*, Winchester (1925)

13. A. W. Goodman, op. cit., p.10

14. Joan Greatrex, op. cit., p.22

15. A. F. Leach, op. cit., p.31

16. Thos. Warton, *History of English Poetry*, London (1778), Vol. II, p.206. Warton gives as his source *Regist. Priorat. St Swithun, Winton*. The source is untraceable and may be fictitious.

17. A. F. Leach, op. cit., p.25

18. A. F. Leach, op. cit., p.31

19. ibid.

20. G. W. Kitchin & T. T. Madge (eds.), *Winchester Cathedral Documents, 1541–1547*, Hants Record Soc., London & Winchester (1889), p.70

21. ibid., p.133

22. Treasurer's Roll of 1541, MS Win. Cath. Lib.

23. ibid., folio 2^v

24. ibid.

25. ibid., folio 11^v

26. G. W. Kitchin & T. T. Madge, op. cit., p.181

27. W. H. Frere (ed.), *Visitation Articles and Injunctions*, London (1910), Vol. III, p.322

28. Florence Goodman (ed.), *Dean Young's Diary*, S.P.C.K., London (1928), p.95

29. Chapter Acts Books, MS Win. Cath. Lib. (hereafter C.A.), May 1596, quoted in Goodman, op. cit., p.12

30. Indenture Matthew Lidford and Dean & Chapter, Ledger Book XII, MS Win. Cath. Lib. folio 33^v

31. 'Mutilated' Treasurer's Roll of 1627, MS Win. Cath. Lib. folio 3^r

32. British Library, MS Lansdown 213. 26–37, folio 351ff., published in *Camden Miscellany* Vol. XVI (1936). See also *Record* (1953), pp.9–15

33. quoted in F. Bussby, *Winchester Cathedral*, Cave, Southampton (1979), p.126

34. F. Bussby, op. cit., p.123

35. N. Wridgway, *Choristers of St George's Chapel*, Slough (1980), pp.19 & 134

36. W. R. W. Stephens & T. T. Madge (eds.), *Winchester Cathedral Documents, 1636–1683*, Hants Record Soc., London & Winchester (1897), pp.21–22

37. A. W. Goodman & W. H. Hutton (eds.), *Winchester Cathedral Statutes*, Oxford (1925), p.53ff.

38. ibid., p.54

39. Chapter Order Book, MS Win. Cath. Lib., 5 April 1683

40. Treasurer's Roll 1683–4, MS Win. Cath. Lib.

41. Treasurer's Roll 1684–5, MS Win. Cath. Lib.

42. Florence Goodman, op. cit., p.141

43. quoted in F. Bussby, op. cit., p.134

Notes to Chapter Two

1. Indenture L. Barrows, Ledger Book XIII, MS Win. Cath. Lib. folio 111ʳ
2. W. R. W. Stephens & T. T. Madge (eds.), *Winchester Cathedral Documents, 1636–1683*, Hants Record Soc., London & Winchester (1897), p.109
3. Treasurer's Rolls 1691–1706, MS Win. Cath. Lib. folio 92ʳff.
4. C.A., 8 June 1666
5. Ch. Order Bk., 29 Nov. 1666
6. Compotus Roll of Will. Payne, Treasurer 1666–7, MS Win. Cath. Lib.
7. C.A., 9 Sept 1678
8. Treasurer's Roll of William Hawkins, 1682–3, MS Win. Cath. Lib.
9. ibid.
10. Ch. Order Bk., 11 Dec. 1667
11. MS Win. Cath. Lib., quoted in F. Bussby *Winchester Cathedral*, Cave, Southampton (1979), pp.157–8
12. Florence Goodman (ed.), *Dean Young's Diary*, SPCK, London (1928), pp.73–4
13. Ch. Order Bk., 11 Dec. 1667
14. Ch. Order Bk., 9 Dec. 1685
15. Ch. Order Bk., 8 Dec. 1693
16. C.A., 25 Nov. 1742
17. quoted in F. Bussby, op. cit., p.186
18. *Dictionary of National Biography*, 'Charles Dibdin'
19. C.A., 24 June 1772
20. C.A., 25 Nov. 1782
21. Patricia Hooper, *William Whiting*, Cave, Southampton (1978), pp.45–6
22. ibid.
23. quoted in A. B. Cook, *About Winchester College*, London (1917)
24. C.A., 25 Nov. 1782
25. C.A., 25 Nov. 1800
26. ibid.
27. C.A., 25 Nov. 1804
28. C.A., 25 June 1809
29. ibid.
30. C.A., 24 March 1814
31. C.A., 23 June 1855
32. C.A., 23 June 1856
33. C.A., 23 June 1812
34. C.A., 25 June 1814
35. C.A., 13 June 1815
36. C.A., 2 Feb. 1815
37. ibid.
38. C.A., 25 Nov. 1818
39. C.A., 24 June 1816
40. C.A., 22 June 1822
41. *The Choristers' Book*, MS Win. Cath. Lib.
42. *Oxford Companion to Music*, article 'Cathedral Music'
43. C.A., 2 Feb. 1815
44. William Cobbett, *Rural Rides*, 23 Oct. 1825
45. C.A., 25 Nov. 1839
46. Patricia Hooper, op. cit., p.28
47. C.A., 29 Sept. 1841
48. 1841 Census, microfilm in Hants County Record Office
49. Patricia Hooper, op. cit., p.33
50. quoted in P. Chappell, *Dr. S. S. Wesley*, London (1977), p.73
51. C.A., 21 Aug. 1849
52. C.A., 5 Oct. 1849
53. *Report of the Ecclesiastical Commissioners*, London (1854)
54. ibid., p.733
55. C.A., 25 Nov. 1856
56. *Hampshire Chronicle*, 6 Dec. 1856, microfilm in Hants County Library
57. C.A., 25 Nov. 1858
58. C.A., 25 Nov. 1859
59. C.A., 25 Nov. 1860
60. paraphrased from C.A., 20 Sept 1861
61. C.A., 23 Feb. 1865
62. C.A., 23 June 1865. Installation of Dr. Geo. Benjamin Arnold
63. *Hampshire Chronicle*, 6 Jan. 1866, microfilm in Hants County Library
64. C.A., 25 Nov. 1869
65. C.A., 23 June 1870
66. *Warrens' Winchester Directory*, 1880, advertisement
67. C.A., 25 Nov. 1873
68. *Memorandum about the Choristers and their School* dated 25 Sept. 1883, MS Win. Cath. Lib., p.4
69. C.A., 23 June 1871
70. C.A., 29 Sept. 1871
71. C.A., 10 Sept. 1878
72. *Memorandum*, (see note 68), p.4
73. C.A., 5 June 1883
74. MS Win. Cath. Lib. One of four surviving letters dated 1882–5
75. quoted in A. W. Goodman, 'The Ancestry of the Pilgrims' School', *Magazine* Vol. I no.10 (1941), p.13
76. C.A., 1 Feb. 1887 and 1 March 1887
77. *Regulations for the Choir Boys* printed under C.A., 6 Jan. 1891
78. I am indebted to Dr. Beatrice Clayre for this information
79. C.A., 30 Dec. 1895
80. C.A., 1 Sept. 1896

INDEX

Numbers in italics refer to the plates

146

149